HEALING: HUMAN AND DIVINE

Healing: Human and Divine

*MAN'S SEARCH FOR HEALTH
AND WHOLENESS THROUGH SCIENCE,
FAITH, AND PRAYER*

EDITED BY

SIMON DONIGER, Ph.D.

ASSOCIATION PRESS · NEW YORK

Library of Congress Catalog Card Number: 57-6889

55

Printed in the United States of America

American Book–Stratford Press, Inc., New York

Preface

Most of the articles embodied in this book have been published during the last seven years in *Pastoral Psychology*, a monthly journal devoted to the integration of the scientific knowledge of human behavior with spiritual and religious values. The Introduction is written by Dr. Earl A. Loomis, Jr., especially for this book. Dr. Loomis is the newly appointed director of the program on Psychiatry and Religion at Union Theological Seminary, and was until recently Professor of Child Psychiatry, and Chief of the Section of Child Development, at the University of Pittsburgh.

The book is divided into four sections. Section 1: Body, Mind, and Spirit, represents the thinking of several outstanding psychiatrists and psychologists who have been deeply concerned with the subject of this

v

volume—man's search for wholeness. Section 2: Religion and Psychiatry, is made up of articles by a group of outstanding theologians who have early in their lives and work become cognizant of, and have been profoundly influenced by, the tremendous contribution of dynamic psychology and psychiatry to our understanding of man, his needs and motivations, and whose work has become a synthesis of the most profound aspects of both theology and psychology.

Section 3: Prayer, is devoted to a spiritual as well as psychological exploration of the meaning of prayer in man's search for both wholeness and relationship to God. Section 4: Spiritual Healing, is a series of studies by some of the most outstanding theologians and psychiatrists in this country, analyzing the deep significance of faith in spiritual healing as distinguished from magic and pure psychotherapy.

The series of articles embodied in this book, though written separately and individually, have obviously a deep and common concern with man's search for wholeness and salvation. It is this common concern which makes out of these separate and individual articles a book of spontaneous and organized purposeful meaning. The editor is deeply grateful to the contributors who have made this book possible.

SIMON DONIGER
Editor

About the Authors

Earl A. Loomis, Jr., M.D., is Director of the Program on Psychiatry and Religion, Union Theological Seminary, formerly Associate Professor of Child Psychiatry, School of Medicine, and Director of the Children's Residential Treatment Service, Western Psychiatric Institute and Clinic, Pittsburgh, Pennsylvania.

John A. P. Millet, M.D., is Consultant to the New York State Department of Mental Hygiene, and Psychiatrist-in-Chief of the American Rehabilitation Committee.

Gotthard Booth, M.D., is Associate, Columbia University Seminar on Religion and Health, New York, and psychiatric adviser to General Theological Seminary and Union Theological Seminary.

Carl R. Rogers is Professor of Psychology, and

Executive Secretary, The Counseling Center, University of Chicago.

Seward Hiltner is Professor of Pastoral Theology, Federated Theological Faculty, University of Chicago, and Pastoral Consultant to *Pastoral Psychology*.

Walter M. Horton is Professor of Theology, Graduate School of Theology, Oberlin College, Oberlin, Ohio.

Ernest E. Bruder is Co-ordinator, Chaplain Services Branch, Saint Elizabeth's Hospital, Department of Health, Education, and Welfare, Washington, D. C., and Editor-in-Chief, *Journal of Pastoral Care*.

Walter G. Muelder is Dean of Boston University School of Theology.

L. Harold De Wolf is Professor of Systematic Theology, Boston University School of Theology.

Paul E. Johnson is Professor of Psychology of Religion, Boston University School of Theology.

George Albert Coe taught for many years as professor at Union Theological Seminary and at Columbia University.

Paul Tillich is University Professor, Harvard Divinity School.

Cyril C. Richardson is Washburn Professor of Church History, Union Theological Seminary.

Wayne E. Oates is Professor of Pastoral Care, Southern Baptist Theological Seminary, Louisville, Kentucky.

Contents

Introduction

THE RAPPROCHEMENT of psychiatry and theology has progressed with an increasing pace over the past decade. What once represented warring or at least mutually suspicious factions now constitute disciplines seeking one another's insights. This hopeful sign in the development of thought and of man's humanity to man is well demonstrated by the articles which fill the pages of this book. The first two sections deal with the similarities and differences of the roles of clergymen and physicians and with the parallel comparisons of their respective fields or disciplines. Section I finds psychiatrists and a psychologist revealing their vital interest in man's nature, his values, and his destiny of self-realization as a person in the fuller context which includes the spiritual. Section II bears testimony to the mature grasp of things psychological by men of the cloth. It is clearly evident in the papers by both groups of authors that they have come a long way from the older psychologies of religion which all too often represented a reduction of faith to science or vice versa. That they have neither "joined 'em or licked 'em," but rather have come into fruitful relation with one another is evident. This point is nicely made by Dr. Horton who sees the twin dangers of "psychologism" and "theologism" and who clarifies some of the confusion through pointing out that while both disciplines use symbols, they are of a different order in each. Yet having distinguished between the approaches to behavior as *sin* (deliberate separation of self from God) or as *symptom* (involuntary and unwitting manifestation of illness) he returns to the holistic conclusion that "to find God, to 'seek first his Kingdom and his righteousness,' and to realize true selfhood, are three distinguishable aspects of *one indivisible process*." (Italics mine.)

The second half of the book is divided on the basis of subject, Section III dealing with prayer from both the psychological and metaphysical sides. In approaching the subject of prayer one is likely to hear at least two rationalistic objections to "objectively efficacious prayer": (1) the possibility of man's having power to manipulate God and hence the temptation to selfish use of prayer poses an ethical objection; and (2) the theory that since God is unchanging not only in his essence but also in his will, and hence that man cannot change or alter God's purpose, design, or plan, constitutes a metaphysical objection. Answers to each of these might be sought. To the first, one might refer to the concept of man's freedom, innate or delegated, which God upholds even at the cost of his own self-limitation. To the second objection—God's unchangeability—one might posit the likelihood that any true communication, encounter, or exchange involves change in *both* parties, that God—to be a true I or Thou of an I-Thou meeting—must also be subject to this experience. If we can get to God at all, in true meeting, we must in some sense both be changed. Therefore after any true meeting neither partner is quite the same again. Jung puts it even more boldly: "The encounter with the creature changes the creator." (*Answer to Job, page 108.*) If grace is to be seen as something other or more than *power, substance,* or general *good will,* then a re-examination of the person and work of the Holy Spirit in the nonverbal, primitive, and basic interpersonal communication between man and man, must be undertaken. Buber's insistence on the fact that God is met at the interfaces of "conversation" between man and man deserves amplification in this context. The role of meditation *and* actional approaches in the making explicit of the implicit and often unconscious communication requires exploration and experimentation before most of the "empirical" aspects of the theology of prayer will find their fullest relevance for the life of man.

Spiritual healing *per se* is the topic of the fourth section. Here it is reviewed in the light of its history and of its relation to science, pastoral psychology, and theology. It is this group of papers which represent in some ways the most daring and advanced of serious and responsible thinking in this area. Much of the groundwork for the concepts herein expressed has been developed in the preceding papers and sections which apply implicitly to healing, health, and wholeness of all types. Yet here the less familiar and currently most challenging possibilities are approached more explicitly.

Reminiscent of Karl Menninger's figure of St. George and Sir Galahad (kill the dragon vs. get the grail) is Bruder's comparison of the questions asked by psychiatrist and by minister: "What is preventing this person from being more loving?" (psychiatrist), and "How can this person utilize his ability to be more loving?" (minister). Again here are two sides of the coin, two principal approaches, yet approaches shared by both disciplines.

In attempting an introduction to this splendid selection of papers on healing, I shall approach the topic from three directions. Healing certainly occurs and no doubt is "here to stay." Yet we lack understanding of its *meaning* and its *modes*. Perhaps before we can acquire understanding of either of these we need to discover and develop a *methodology* for its study.

For some, of course, the *meaning* of healing is that it

is a message of comfort, of solace, and of reassurance against the overwhelmingly disturbing problem of evil and pain. If indeed the forces for health are stronger than those for illness, then God is on our side and so is nature; and this gives man both as believer and as physician the courage and conviction that it is worth going on in the face of what may seem to be overwhelming odds in the present. This *sign* of God's ultimate conquest of evil or of its ultimate defeat as a leading theme is of course eschatological in implication.

For others, healing holds magical portent. It reveals the power of man to move nature and God for man's betterment (sometimes, too, for God's greater glory). It is interesting to compare the different uses of the word and concept "magic" by the various authors. For Tillich, much of faith healing is magic; and, for Booth, much of the popular and current tone of science is magically derived. A full treatment of the meaning of magic for modern man is called for. Perhaps one of our authors will follow through and fulfill this need.

The *modes* of healing discussed in this book range far. Dramatic miracle in the face of despair with the order of nature and human nature is not ignored. Yet most of our authors place much more emphasis on nature in the service of God and of man's need rather than upon God as the reverser of nature's ways to suit man's whim or urgency. N. P. Williams' reminder of

Augustine's dictum could well be restressed in this context: ". . . grace is to be upheld not in disparagement of nature, but as that which liberates . . . nature." (*The Grace of God*, page 113.) Yet reference to "the orderly and predictable" universe, to the *vis medicatrix naturae*, and to the "miraculous-in-the-commonplace" somehow begs the question of the really unique or at least nearly unique events which cannot be predicted, repeated, or produced on demand. The latter, which defy the ken of both mechanistic views of experimental science and magical views of healing and prayer, cannot be brushed aside as nonexistent, though as Richardson insists, they are both in fact and by definition rare. Pragmatically this rarity may tend to cast doubt on the relevance of the phenomenon—and in this connection, I as a physician cannot resist congratulating the authors for avoiding the pitfall of implying that miraculous cures are available as a substitute for competent medical diagnosis and treatment. (This is not to deny on my part any of the enthusiasm I feel for the value of *faith* in doctor, patient, and community—faith which can strengthen, mobilize, and potentiate the healing forces from all sources. We can be grateful that most of us have left behind the either/or which excludes multiple causation—or better, *multiple interaction* in the healing process.)

Coming finally to the need for a *methodology* for studying the phenomenon of healing I feel we are at our weakest. This is not to disparage either healing itself or our outstanding panel of authors. Rather it is to underscore the deficiency in current scientific, and indeed philosophic, method when it comes to dealing with the intensely personal, the spiritual, and the unique. Some scientists have gone so far as to admit that they are uninterested in unpredictable, unreproducible events; some philosophers question that such events have meaning. Yet this looking askance has not deterred either healers or healees. There is more enthusiasm for this very subject today than in anyone's memory of time past. Admittedly we cannot rely on anecdotal healing accounts as literally and objectively valid. Yet the accounts are events in themselves and events to be examined. Furthermore, the events behind the accounts deserve thorough study. This has been difficult in the past since the best of healers frequently fear (rightly or wrongly) that their power will disappear if and when it is too closely examined. Perhaps if the *attitude* of both examiner and examinee were to change, then the examination could proceed. Neither the attitude of suspicion nor wish-fulfillment gullibility are likely to lead to answers, but trust, respect, and concern for all involved are essential.

But going beyond attitudes, important as these are, we still have but the flimsiest rudiments of methodology on which to go if we are to investigate and verify, analyze and clarify what we mean by healing. I am not here speaking of an attempt to communicate what is going on, to compare healers, healing communities, healees, healing climates, healing periods in history, and so on. Such comparisons need not destroy the possibility, nay probability, of uniqueness of the events, provided one concedes two postulates: (1) that possibly healing might come to anyone provided the conditions (whatever those may be) were met, and (2) that though healing might be different in each person healed, it still could represent in each person something else in another person. There might well be profit in studying the make-up and motives of those who seek to be healers, to be healed, or to observe healing feats.

Beginnings of such methodologies have of course appeared in social psychology researches. The Q-Technique of Stephenson is only one of several possibilities providing for comparison where linear measurement is unavailable, or more often unavailing. Yet beyond the searching methodological tools which I am sure the more sophisticated researchers can unearth and apply, or rather behind and before them, is the caution: adequate medical responsibility must be assumed, accurate observations and records must be made, and conviction must not be confused with fact. This has been the great caution of the Medical Bureau at Lourdes, which for years has been charged with the simple but all-important task of ascertaining whether or not something alleged actually happened. Regrettably their positive data are limited in number because most if not all of their studies are *done after the fact.* In other words, after someone is healed they begin to study the history, previous medical and laboratory examinations, and other pertinent data. If these are ambiguous or incomplete the case is of course not certified as miraculous, or rather, as inexplicable through known medical principles. No one knows in how many cases thus unavailable for investigation or comparison real healing had actually occurred.

In fine, and to hark back to *meaning*, Tillich rightly reminds us that simple physical health here and now is not the end and goal of human life, that mortality is our lot, and that there are fates worse than sickness and death. Perhaps healing must be viewed more globally, less as a simple transmutation of tissues or humors, more as an outcome or consummation in which sickness and its erstwhile attendant evils no longer have dominion over a man. Perhaps, sometimes, to be healed is to pass from death into life, even if it be from a living death in this life into another but new and deathless life.

BODY, MIND, AND SPIRIT

Body, Mind, and Spirit

Science Based on Mechanistic Solutions Leaves
Us Bewildered; Religion Which Denies Man's
Biological Nature Commands
a Dubious Loyalty

Even the most dogmatic of men would hardly claim to hold all the keys to those secrets that lie hidden in our human frames, whether they be the many unknowns in our physical constitution, the even more inexplicable processes that seem to us to be basically a part of our mental field, or the various manifestations of the opposing principles of good and evil, both in attitudes and behavior, which are generally recognized as having some other source than the physical constitution or the mental apparatus—a source which can best be designated by the word "spirit." It would indeed require omniscience to elaborate the interconnections of these elements in human nature,

23

and to explain the obstinate prejudices, the innumerable contradictions, the absurd follies or the incredible courage which at one time or another are observable in the feelings, thoughts, and actions of individuals and groups.

Every individual who enters a professional calling is motivated by needs within himself which he rarely completely understands. I feel that I can speak with some conviction on this point, since in the course of over thirty-five years' study of human beings, this impression has become increasingly easy of verification through the assembling of fact in the developmental lives of some thousands of patients.

In my own particular branch of medical practice, which I prefer to call psychoanalytic medicine, it has become a quite general observation that those who enter it are motivated in the main by an intense curiosity as to the mainsprings of human personality. This curiosity stems from uncertainties as to their own nature, their problems, their conflicts, their anxieties, and their values. The thesis that nobody can understand the psychoanalytic method without undergoing a personal analysis is second in significance only to the conclusion that nobody is fitted for treating human beings with the techniques of psychoanalytic therapy unless he has been properly prepared for the work by a thorough personal analysis and by an adequate system of supervision during the early years of his practice.

Modern medical practice at the best level takes full cognizance of the fact that the human being must be considered as a total entity, not just as someone who has a bad pair of tonsils, a grumbling appendix, or a low basal metabolism. Modern medicine further- more considers such established diagnoses as diabetes, asthma, eczema, colitis, duodenal ulcer, high blood pressure, and others, as more than localized disorders of some bodily organ, be it the pancreas, the bronchi- oles, the skin, the colon, the duodenum, or the blood- vessels.

Modern medicine looks upon these illnesses from two standpoints, first as sources of impaired function- ing, often causing severe discomfort, and not infre- quently threatening life, which call for the best emer- gency care that can be provided. Second, modern medicine views these disorders as a break in the adap- tive efficiency of the human machine.

In order to increase the efficacy of the emergency treatment, and to prepare safeguards against recur- rences, the significance of the illness to the patient, the pressures under which he has lived, the attitudes of those nearest him, his economic and social situation, and the outstanding traits in his personality—all these, and perhaps other special factors must be evaluated, and their contribution to the total picture of disability must be correctly estimated. If this is not done the adrenalin may check the asthma, the ointment relieve the eczema, and the diet heal the ulcer, but the whole patient is little altered and the same break in his adaptive efficiency may well occur again.

These new insights have led to the coining of the term psychosomatic medicine. This term does not imply the arrival of a new specialty in the medical family, but symbolizes the full recognition by medical science of the interdependence of physical and mental events in producing an integrated or healthy organism, and the corollary proposition that a disturbance of this integration in either the mental or the physical field can produce an upset in the adaptive equilibrium leading to an amazing variety of symptoms.

Medical science, therefore, has reluctantly consented to abandon the simpler task of investigating the human organism as a mechanic examines an automobile which breaks down on the highway. Long neglect of the mental apparatus by clinicians who were impressed by discoveries in the fields of tissue pathology, bacteriology, and biological chemistry, led naturally to the flourishing of cults of various kinds whose exponents were often successful in relieving disorders of function which defied the nostrums prescribed by medical practitioners.

Disturbances of equilibrium producing bodily as well as mental symptoms were too often treated as though only the bodily discomforts merited the attention of the physician, while the mental components of the disorder were given short shrift, with such admonitions as "There is nothing really much the matter with you," or "This is only your nerves," or "The trouble with you is that you think too much about yourself," or "You worry altogether too much." Such admonitions tended only to make the patient feel guilty, disappointed, more anxious, and frequently resentful, and rendered him an easy victim of the wiles of the unscrupulous.

It is a curious fact that the man who through his endlessly painstaking investigations laid the cornerstone of this new orientation of medical science to the study of the whole man, began his professional life in the field of neurological research. While already conspicuous for his work on the pathology of the nervous system, Sigmund Freud became interested in the phenomenon of hypnosis. His classical work on the interpretation of dreams was published at the turn of the century. The antagonism with which his discoveries were greeted by his medical colleagues and by large sections of the intelligentsia was typical of the resistance of orthodox thinkers to any revolutionary discovery which threatens their continuing prestige. This battle, however, is largely a matter of the past, since modern psychiatry is now firmly rooted in the science of psychodynamics, of which Freud must be considered the founder, though laboratory workers, notably psychologists, through their experimental work, have brought invaluable evidence to support and clarify many of the findings of psychological investigators.

So much then for the now generally accepted thesis that the mind and body of man cannot be considered as separate and independent entities when the nature of the human organism is the subject under consideration, whether in a state of health or suffering from some disorder. What can be said then from the standpoint of the medical man, and particularly the medical specialist who devotes his time to the study and treatment of disorders which are reflected in the mental field, in regard to the spirit of man? What do such words as "spiritual" mean to him? What is his position with regard to religious influences? How does he think about such phenomena as conversion? Does he believe in free will? What are his value systems?

To answer any of these questions thoughtfully and completely would require a series of treatises of some length. I do not, however, want to dodge the questions and must attempt some kind of answer to them, which, as a radio commentator might say, "does not necessarily reflect the opinions of my colleagues." In fact, each of my colleagues would have his answer, because each has had a different experience from the other, and has been more or less influenced by his scientific thinking as well as by a variety of extrinsic factors in his personal life. Each has his private, personal, and special outlook which is the peculiar essence of the human being, that basic difference from his fellows derived from the infinite permutations and combinations of physical, emotional, and intellectual variants which comprise personality. Each is characterized by his own particular form of struggle toward a total expression of the self which he would find satisfying and satisfactory.

This struggle is the essence of the individual human being. The word "spirit," derived as it is from the Latin word *spiritus*, means "breath." The mystery of the individual can never be entirely explained in terms of physical constitution plus emotional tendencies plus intellectual organization. The religious hypothesis that this basic individual essence which differentiates each of us from his fellows, is the gift of God antedates history in its origins, and finds some kind of expression in the writings of all religious authorities.

For the medical man life begins when the infant takes his first breath. The air is breathed in—the spirit of life enters. From that time on, the child becomes a more or less independent unit whose vital processes are self-regulating and not dependent on the vital processes of another human being, its mother. The die is cast. The individual passes gradually from the stage of helpless dependence to the period of full maturity and independence. By the age of sixteen or thereabouts he is possessed of all the essentials for self-determination, and his future development will be determined by the adaptive patterns which he forms in his struggle for existence and fulfillment.

The most complicated of all the bodily systems and the least fully explored is the nervous system. The brain of man is noteworthy for the fact that although certain parts of it can be definitely shown to govern certain functions, there are large areas whose exact functions remain to be defined. The brain is the great co-ordinator of all bodily functions, as well as the mediator of all energies which appear as mental activity. Aside from disease, injury, or defective development there are no forces that impede its successful operations more effectively than anxiety. It might be said that the mastery of anxiety is one of the most significant tasks which the human being has to accomplish if he is to be a free agent in pursuing his aims.

Since the human brain is chiefly characterized, as compared with the brains of the primates, by the vastly greater proportion of the forebrain to the total volume of the organ, it is reasonable to suppose that the mysteries of human individuality are locked in the secret functions of this portion of the brain substance. It is now generally recognized that the so-called higher functions of the personality are resident in the frontal lobes. Extensive damage to these areas may interfere but slightly with bodily functioning and with those responses which have become largely automatic, whereas it is always followed by disturbances of social attitudes and purposive behavior. The vast nexus of association tracts in the cortex are doubtless responsible for the vastly greater understanding of his environment, both physical and social, which the human being possesses.

From this capacity springs the understanding of interpersonal relationships and the need to act in such ways as to achieve feelings of security in relation to other human beings. Identification of the self with others becomes the mainspring of ethical striving. No human being can find fulfillment in his pattern of adaptation unless this need is recognized and a channel for its expression is discovered and utilized. The mysterious power which the human being possesses of projecting himself into a future and nonexisting situation, the power of the imagination, makes it possible for him to plan his adaptations in advance including those which have to do with his relationships to his fellows.

In the earliest years of man's history his enemies were the elements and the wild beasts. Though he has never entirely succeeded in establishing a symbiotic relationship with these ancient enemies, his adaptive resources have enabled him to provide stout bulwarks against them. These afford him sufficient security to allow increasing freedom of movement and wider areas for adventure and experimentation. He has, however, never succeeded in erecting reliable defenses against his principal enemy, his fellow man.

In limited areas on the surface of the globe man is now able to live in relative security in the company of his fellows, but the symbiotic equilibrium is notoriously unstable, and no perfect device, no universally acceptable technique, has as yet been developed to overcome this social instability. It would seem at the present writing that this devastating failure of man to solve the chief threat to his continuing existence and progress has reached an all-time high. His imagination is tortured by visions of a return to chaos, and excited by too faltering hopes that his new machinery of insight may be of a substance solid enough to withstand all impacts of his own destructive energies.

The Devil is at large in a big way: his penchant for persuading gullible man is too familiar to need comment. If a finger is put firmly upon his horns, his hooves kick up a new disturbance at some other spot. He is less tangible than mercury, and far less manageable. The Devil is the symbolic embodiment of all those negative forces in the unexplored unconscious of man which threaten his freedom—his doubts, his fears, his ruthless power drives, his cruelty, his hates, his suspicions. The concept of equilibrium of forces, however, demands that for each force there be an opponent. Consequently, there can be no Devil without God.

Just as man is beset by these forces of destruction, so too he is propelled constantly forward by his striving toward constructive synthesis. It is this force which lies behind his stumbling efforts toward the creation of harmonious groupings. The history of such efforts begins with the family, continues with the tribe, is carried on through the birth of nations, is expressed in the concept of the commonwealth, and finds its ultimate symbol in the charter of the United Nations. In the religious sense, these are some of the ways in which man expresses his Godlike purposes.

No progress toward an effective synthesis can be expected unless this basic principle of antagonistic forces is comprehended and accepted. A simple example can be seen in the delicate operations of the human hand. If it were not for the opposing tendencies toward flexion and extension, functions inherent in opposing muscle groups, no single delicate manipulation of objects would be possible. The same principle applies in the field of interpersonal relations, where the needs of one individual impinge upon the needs of his opposite number.

Too frequently those of the first, being of egocentric origin, if given full and free expression, would interfere with the realization of the other's needs. If there is a partial sacrifice or suppression of such energies by one party there is a decrease in the resistance from the other party and an increased freedom for the expression of his energies. From such an arrangement of forces a joint and participating relationship becomes possible and a new dynamic potential is released. One need hardly carry this argument further, since it is equally applicable to individual and opposing muscle groups and to the various groupings within the human family. Democracy is rooted in the two-party system.

The observations of Freud and his followers are chiefly significant from the fact that the truths which they made known were brought together and assembled in a systematic and scrupulous manner, thus making possible the elaboration of new theories of human behavior. No scientist was ever more careful than Freud in distinguishing observation from deduction and deduction from theory. No investigator was ever more conscientious, albeit at times reluctant, to abandon theoretical formulations, when they failed to explain facts, no more courageous in formulating further theories.

The various splinter movements that have occurred in the field of psychoanalytic thinking and professional organization have created some confusion in the minds of the lay public. This has been accentuated by the wide publicity given to differences in theoretical formulations. Such differences, however, are inevitable in any field of scientific inquiry, and fertilize the field for further growth. The worst compliment that psychoanalysts of today could pay to the memory of Freud would be to abandon the testing and retesting of theoretical formulations, no matter what their source. The greatest tribute, on the other hand, would be the continuous retesting of his hypotheses, the restatement of facts derived from his observations, and the development of new theories to be further tested by the techniques of scientific inquiry.

Among the challenging legacies which Freud left to his colleagues were his repeated statements that despite everything that is known about neurosis its fundamental origins are still unknown. Such a statement, however, does not imply that neurosis cannot be successfully treated. There are parallels in medical history for this apparently contradictory situation, including, for example, the successful use of quinine in malaria which long antedated the discovery of the plasmodium. Among his latest reflections was his interest in the unexplained phenomenon of extrasensory perception. It is well to recognize, therefore, that Freud was not the founder of a new system of authoritarian belief, nor the high priest of a new cult, but a great challenger of superstition and a promoter of more serious searching for the mainsprings of human behavior, in its healthy and unhealthy manifestations.

The aim of psychoanalytic treatment is essentially very simple, to relieve the ego, the consciously operating part of the personality, from those anxieties which hamper its most effective functioning. Anxiety is simply the signal which warns us of danger, and apprises us of the fact that we are in need of taking the measures to meet it. The danger may come from one of three main sources—our primitive emotions, our restrictive inner prohibitions, or the demands of the people with whom we are associated. Such a classification leaves out, of course, the threat of physical dangers—such as earthquakes, lightning, and tempest. These do not threaten our self-estimate, but our physical existence, and with rare exceptions we are able to take appropriate measures to remove the danger.

At this point it will be well to define the term "restrictive inner prohibitions." These "thou shalt nots" are static formulas which we acquire in earliest childhood, and represent the internalized attitudes of our parents. They stay with us as a sort of inner Gestapo which is constantly on the lookout for the escape of forbidden wishes of which the ego might be tempted to take advantage. The rule of this Gestapo may be so arbitrary and exacting that the ego spends most of its time and thought in making sure that its orders are being observed. This may be called the "infantile conscience."

Although it is distantly related to the adult conscience it bears little more than a family resemblance to it. Instead of providing the ego with a reasonable guide to action it is constantly threatening it with the possibility of disaster if it attempts to take any steps that might be emotionally gratifying. One of the chief tasks of the mature ego is to learn to differentiate between the infantile conscience (or superego) and the adult conscience (or ego-ideal). The activity of the former can be detected when the ego feels anxious with respect to some action it contemplates: when the adult conscience is in action the ego feels supported and encouraged.

By now it becomes apparent that the psychoanalyst views the ego as the executive officer in the government of personality. Its function is to listen to all the points of view which various lobbies of conflicting interest lay before it. It has to weigh these demands and must necessarily be governed in its final decision by its own experience and current sense of values. From the standpoint of investigative science psychoanalysis may be said to have no absolute value beyond that of seeking further clues to the mysteries of human nature. From the standpoint of a therapeutic technique it is motivated by the same ideals as those which motivate all human beings who wish to be of service to others.

It is as much a fallacy to say that the psychoanalyst is a lifeless sounding board against which the frustrations and anxieties of the patient are bounced and returned to the sender, as it is to assume that he influences his patient to get rid of all his inhibitions so that he can feel free to express himself "all over the place" in every way that gives him selfish enjoyment. Psychoanalysis as a therapeutic technique involves a very particular sort of long-continued co-operation, with a view to the removal of those anxieties which prevent an individual from achieving fullness of life, and approaching more closely his own ego-ideal.

The formation of a conscious and healthy ego-ideal has often been prevented by unhappy beginnings, and the anxiety which brings the patient to the therapist may be rooted in this very frustration. The psychoanalyst respects the right of the individual to decide his own fate. He aims to help him face the realities both of his feelings and of the situations which he has to meet. Although he avoids taking responsibility for his patient's decisions, his own sense of values inevitably is sensed by the patient during the therapeutic experience. He becomes, or should become, the promoter and supporter, strong enough, through better understanding of conflicting motivations, to withstand these inner pressures, and so to arrive at decisions which represent a dynamic integration of forces, and make possible more effective behavior. Since the human being does not exist in a social vacuum, such behavior to be more effective must necessarily involve more appropriate relations with his fellow man.

I trust that I shall not fall into the error of misinterpreting the term spirit in its religious significance. From my own standpoint, however, it seems applicable to that feeling of urgency in man to struggle toward an integration of his mental and physical self in the direction of some ideal, an ideal whose pursuit will result in a decreasing burden of anxiety, a more effective social role, and a deep respect for the eternal mysteries which the finite and limited nature of man can never be expected to penetrate.

It is here that religion has the opportunity to fulfill its best function. It may be that the time has come for a new formulation of the aims of religion, for a more inspired leadership, based on appreciating the needs of man in his new setting, the setting of the Atomic Age. This is no time for regression to outworn types of religious pronouncements, which modern man can no longer accept. Never before has there been a time when religion and science needed more generally to recognize that this is not the time for civil war.

Their aims though not identical are to a large degree mutually complementary. The approach of science is not apparently dependent on belief, even though scientists do believe certain assumptions which further observations or discoveries later may prove to be untenable and deceptive. The approach of religion is frankly based on faith, on belief in the triumph of good over evil, on the existence of the Creator, who ordained the nature and relations of things, including the transient existence of man. Science which is only interested in mechanistic solutions leaves its exponents bewildered and frustrated; religion which lays down laws that deny the biological truths of human nature commands a dubious loyalty.

The common ground on which science and religion can meet without procedural complications is the ground of promoting a more complete understanding of the causes of unrest and conflict in the lives of human beings, and of using their particular approaches to these problems with due regard to the importance of other avenues to insight. The social sciences, among which I number psychiatry, can point to the factors which prevent men from realizing their potentialities to the fullest extent possible, and may help human beings to remove or achieve mastery over such obstacles; religion can provide the conviction that the goals of such effort are worth the struggle that is put forth.

GOTTHARD BOOTH, M.D.

Basic Concepts of Psychosomatic Medicine

Illness Is a Reminder of the Purpose of Life [1]

THE CONCEPT AND PHASE "psychosomatic medicine" mark the end of the phase in Western civilization during which body and soul were believed to be substantially different: one gross matter following mechanistic laws, the other immaterial spirit potentially free, but during life more or less completely imprisoned in the body. Empirical medicine, as it progressed in the use of mechanical, physical, and chemical methods, became aware of the fact that a certain number of cases did not react as expected, according to the laws of physiology. In some such cases psychological conflicts were obviously of influence. Some psychiatrists, such as Jung, even added the concept of a specific psychological energy to the forms of energy known from physics. The first step toward psychosomatic medi--

[1] (All footnotes appear at the end of chapters.)

cine was the demand that each case be studied for physical *and* for psychological pathology. Such studies found that 60 per cent of the cases of stomach ulcer had a weak stomach and a normal soul, while 40 per cent had a psychopathic soul which made the normal stomach sick.

About simultaneously with this development in medicine, physics arrived at a new concept of the world. Studying the behavior of atoms minutely, physicists found the old dichotomy of matter and mind an illusion. Two discoveries were of particular significance:

1. Rutherford discovered that there is no matter which *contains* various forms of energy, but that the physical world is identical with electrical energy; electrons which, like solar systems, operate in empty space.

2. Planck found that the electrons do not follow immutable, deterministic laws. The immutable laws of classical physics had been derived from experiments with large groups of electrons and under specific, simplified conditions. The individual electron behaves in an absolutely unpredictable manner. The more complex the structure of the electron system, the more significant the freedom of the electrons becomes.

Schroedinger, a physicist, recently analyzed the facts of heredity from the point of view of atomic physics. His findings should be mentioned, because they illustrate the qualities of fate and of freedom which are inherent in living organisms. The constancy of living forms through the succeeding generations is transmitted through the genes. Each gene is a big and relatively stable molecule. A certain number of them change from time to time due to the irregular behavior of the electrons composing the molecule. Thus the genes of contemporary horseshoe crabs have not changed for millions of years. The genes of some horseshoe crab, however, did change millions of years ago, and this broke the chain of apparent determinism. A new step in evolution had taken place, with many more to follow until man joined creation.

Similarly in human brains most of the processes go on the same way as they did thousands of years ago, and in all of us alike. Yet a certain number of the processes are different for large groups of individuals, such as the various constitutional types. Finally in each individual at times unique and unpredictable processes take place. The functioning of our organs and our actions and reactions toward the world are identical with the electronic processes. They represent the metrical aspects of what constitutes in our unconscious and conscious lives, growth, experience, aspiration, and decision. There is no borderline between the material and the immaterial parts of the living organism, between somatic and psychological realities. The only valid distinction to be made is the distinction between what we can interpret psychologically, and what we do not understand. Under the influence of psychoanalysis we have experienced a steady widening of our knowledge about the psychological significance of our organs and of their diseases. All body organs form part of our personality.

Before going into the specific concepts of psychosomatic medicine I shall give you a somewhat detailed description of a particular disease. I have chosen Parkinsonism for various reasons; partly because I made a special study of it, partly because it is relatively rare and therefore not likely to involve people subjectively. It is also a relatively modern disease and it highlights certain problems of our age. As to basic principles, there is no qualitative difference between Parkinsonism and other diseases as far as psychology goes. There are no "psychosomatic diseases" as one still reads in professional and popular articles and books. The old idea of "normal people with a sick body" and of "psychopathic people with a healthy body" has to be abandoned. There are only healthy and sick personalities.

From the traditional point of view Parkinsonism appeared to be a tragic accident. Until the disease process becomes manifest, the individual has usually been a particularly normal individual in his physical and psychological aspects. Then, without provocation, his muscles become more and more rigid, his posture and extremities become bent. Hands and feet are in a constant tremor which stops only during sleep or while some willful action takes place. The longer the disease lasts the fewer actions are possible. Eventually the patient becomes completely paralyzed. The anatomical study of the brain reveals that certain areas of the brain have degenerated. Judged from the point of view that disease is the result of some abnormality, there was no explanation, either physical or psychological, which could explain why this particular patient contracted Parkinsonism.

Psychosomatic medicine taught us to look more closely into the lives of patients. It studied the biography of people not for what went wrong, but with an impartial interest in what specifically happened to them.

In the case of the future Parkinsonian we find that he *inherited* a constitutional disposition toward action. Not only did he show preference for using his muscles, but also for enterprise in general. In comparison to his brothers and sisters he applied himself more strenuously to his work. Furthermore, he tried to identify himself with the domineering one of his two parents. All this, for reasons which I have given in medical papers previously, must be considered the result of an inherited disposition. Other influences in the life of the later Parkinsonian seem to be *external accidents;* the domineering parent happened to be a moralist. Furthermore, as a child he was in a competitively weak position regarding his brothers and sisters; the last one of a great number of siblings, an ugly

duckling among good-looking ones; the parents suffered economic setbacks at a critical point of his development. The combination of all these tendencies
and circumstances accounts for a personality who is
bound to succeed, because he is anxious to improve his
performance and position. At the same time he is not
an ordinary go-getter, but scrupulously honest, and
ready to give up his own advantage for some moral
purpose. This adds to his external success the reputa-
tion of having an angelic character.

All this development finally reaches the critical
point where the quasi-religious concern with success
meets with defeat; either external difficulties have become excessive, or the inner vitality has been reduced
by age or conflicts. At this point the disease process
begins. Its essence is that the personality regresses from
realistic satisfactions to a level of merely symbolical
satisfactions. In his years of health the individual pro-
ceeded from action to action with a feeling of freedom. He *wanted* to act. In the course of the disease
the patient becomes more and more the victim of biological tendencies which force him to act. The kind
of activity into which he is forced must be considered
a caricature of his original personality; his muscles are
in a state of constant tension, and hands and legs are
shaking. The whole body is kept in a rigid position.
The shaking increases when an attempt is made to stop
it by force. The old tendency to assume the dominat-
ing role is also evident in the fact that the patient may

be completely unable to move on command, but act normally under the influence of emotions or in his sleep. The anxiety about success appears in the fact that the patient is unable to try such actions with which he failed once. Each failure restricts his range of initiative more and more as he is more weighted down by shame on account of past failures.

Eventually the patient may become completely bedridden and dependent on external help. But even in this state the need for domination persists; he expects to be helped exactly according to his individual expectations, just as he had given help previously according to his own individual standards. He is hard to please because his behavior had not been motivated by sympathy with others, but by moral judgment. To the environment it often appears incomprehensible how such an active, ambitious, individual can possibly bear his helpless condition. If one analyzes the character of the disease symptoms, however, it becomes obvious that they satisfy the basic tendencies of the individual on a symbolic level. More than in his days of health the fully developed Parkinsonian is the very image of a rigid man, impatiently bent on action. His masklike face denies subjective feelings, his steady gaze suggests that he is concerned exclusively with the goal of his contemplated action.

In our Western culture we are too inclined to assume that what man desires most of all is realistic satisfaction of an increasing number of objective needs. It seems therefore highly significant that the deeper biological tendencies of the organisms are more intent on maintaining the dynamic orientation of the personality than on material satisfactions. When the specific personality development is frustrated in the outer world, the outer world is sacrificed rather than the individual attitude. In order to maintain the latter the patient expresses it symbolically, accepting at the same time pain and frustration in his object relationships.

The treatment of the Parkinsonian proceeds on two levels:

1. By means of drugs the balance in the nervous system can be changed in favor of a more relaxed functioning of the motor system.

2. The influence of the physician can be brought to bear on the personality orientation of the patient. The physician attempts to bring the patient to insight into the one-sided character of his past unthinking system of values. On the other hand, he is relieved from his deep feelings of shame by being made to understand that his disability is as honorable as a wound received in a just war. On the other hand, he is made conscious that action, success, and morality are not the supreme values of human existence, but that charity and acceptance of others are values without which human existence would be impossible. Such strengthening of neglected sides of the personality is partly

achieved by verbal suggestion. It is more important, however, that the physician himself act according to his words; he must be free from anxiety regarding his own success. Any suggestion that the physician considers improvement as a result of his or the patient's being "good," is likely to bring a relapse into paralyzed moralistic anxieties.

I hope that the details of this particular disease process will give a more concrete background to the following remarks which will be concerned with a formulation of the principles of psychosomatic medicine.

First of all, I wish to stress the importance of the individual personality structure. Under the influence of democratic ideology, medicine and psychology have been too emphatic about "common human nature," about the difference between "normal" and "abnormal" people. Though it is a fact that each human being is equipped with the same organs and functions, they actually play very different roles in different human beings. The different body types have been found to be associated with specific personality types. I mentioned before that for the adjustment of the later Parkinsonian the motor system played a predominant role from childhood on. People who later become subject to high blood pressure have a very different attitude; they do not rely on action so much, but rather on their capacity for identification with the cultural group. An aggressively dependent attitude seems to characterize the later sufferer from stomach ulcers.

The personality patterns associated with different organ systems are not easily detected. It is easy to distinguish psychotic personalities, but in most diseases there is no gross mental pathology, only variations of intensity. Such typical variations can be found only by comparison of large groups of patients and by use of objective personality tests. So far there has been increasing evidence that disease always befalls the function which has been leading in the personality orientation. People are capable of standing a great deal of frustration as long as it concerns a function not particularly valuable to the individual, be it feeding, or activity, or sex. Sexual frustration plays an important role for the neurotic type, but not for most schizophrenics.

Disease befalls the leading function at the point where it is frustrated by the life situation. The organ carrying the leading function becomes affected, first functionally and finally structurally. The relationship between disease and the dominant function is very important. In the mechanistic period of medicine disease was explained as the result of organ weakness. Actually the opposite is true; the strongest function is likely to become the victim of disease. "The first will be the last. . . ." The principle which underlies the organ selection of disease was first discovered in the field of psychiatry. Jung found that neurosis and psychosis occur when the most differentiated function of the individual becomes ineffective, as in the case of a brilliant thinker who is faced with a situation which requires feeling, or an empiricist in a situation which requires intuition. Under these circumstances the formerly leading function becomes unconscious; and the underdeveloped, neglected function is forced into action. Since the underdeveloped function is likely to be on a childish level, the situation usually remains unsolved and the differentiated function stays paralyzed. An example of this underdeveloped function is the Parkinsonian with his underdeveloped sympathy which makes the formerly angelic person an ungracious patient.

Although the formerly leading function becomes ineffective with respect to practical purposes, the disease process maintains it in the center of the personality orientation. In the days of health the individual is hardly conscious of his particular orientation. It seems natural to him to be active, acquisitive, possessive, or whatever it may have been. He assumes that everybody is this way and that something is wrong with those who are too obviously different. In the days of illness, however, conscious attention is focused on the diseased function and its representative organ. Thus the function finds satisfaction symbolically, although its satisfaction means practical defeat.

To sum up the principles of pathogenesis: disease occurs when the representative organ function fails to meet the demands of the life situation. The disease organ satisfies the original attitude of the personality on a symbolical level. Previously neglected functions become the leading ones, but in a primitive form. Disease thus is part of a compensating process in which the first becomes the last, and the last the first.

Treatment of disease can be attempted in two fundamentally different ways: The frustrating situation can eventually be changed in favor of the leading function. This would make realistic satisfaction possible once more. At short range this principle may be expedient, but it leaves the patient in danger of running into the same situation again later on. This is most likely in the case of the more serious chronic ailments, because the individual has usually built for himself a one-sided life situation which amounts to a formidable trap.

The more constructive treatment attempts a new orientation of the personality. Previously neglected sides of the personality are brought into the foreground, the old favored side is recognized in its limitations.

Sometimes this reorientation takes place spontaneously, often in the form of a conversion experience. Under the impact of the disease the sick may become intuitively aware of the limitations of his past life. In cases where the patient becomes religious, skeptics often suspect a utilitarian motive, a wish to propitiate God and thus to gain magic help. I feel that there is no reason for sneering at such conversions, even where they are to some extent insincere. The fact of the re-orientation itself contains an element of valid experience.

Conversion comes close to the problem of *sacrifice* in its relationship to health. Religious practices all over the world have developed the idea of sacrifice; the voluntary surrender of something valuable to the deity. When we realize the danger of one-sided overdevelopment for the individual, we recognize that voluntary sacrifice of an overvalued function may be an effective method of warding off the involuntary sacrifice brought through disease. In our Western culture there is the particular danger of one-sided development, because it is so much concerned with the worship of progress and competition. It easily seduces man to concentrate on the one function which is best developed in him and therefore most apt to be useful in his competitive struggle. Against this tendency Christianity has urged the concept that pride is the greatest sin. Although at short range the pursuit of pride seems to be more rewarding in this world, the long-range view sees the principles of spiritual and of worldly health in agreement.

The services and sacraments of the Church appear to be related particularly to the neglected and unde-

veloped side of the Western man which is concerned
with his existence as a human being beyond the limitations of his specific and overemphasized individuality.
The symbolic equality of participation in the services
of the Church seems to me the positive counterpart to
the sacrifice of pride, as demanded by Christian ethics.

The sick are particularly in need of this experience
of relatedness. As has been discussed previously, the
very fact of sickness denotes that the individual has
stressed his specific and unique individuality so much
that he defeated himself in terms of the world of everyday reality. Thus he is isolated from ordinary human
fellowship, but he is also spiritually isolated by the one-
sidedness and anxiety in which he tried to succeed by
relying on his own strength and endowment. Communion and unction are sacraments in which the consciousness of the sick and isolated individual is drawn
back into the experience of his basic humanity and
common relatedness to God. In this way he may become able to use those sides of his personality which he
had neglected because they did not serve the purposes of his ego. He may gather strength for recovery
for a new life, or he may at least become reconciled.

To sum up the principles of psychosomatic therapy,
the individual may be helped by adjusting the external
situation in favor of his frustrated attitude. At least in
the case of seriously sick personalities, the value of
this method is limited. The physician must answer the

question: does the consciously frustrated side of the personality deserve charity, or rather the side which the individual had neglected in the past? More often the latter seems to be the case. With the exception of the rare cases of spontaneous conversion, rational psychotherapy and religious means can be effective.

It would appear that religion and science are becoming more and more able to speak the same language and to bend their efforts in the same direction. This justifies the expectation of an improvement of therapeutic results for those cases where priest and physician co-operate. I am under the impression that to some extent those expectations are fulfilled increasingly. On the other hand, I consider it dangerous optimism to add psychosomatic medicine to the numerous political and sociological schemes by which the millennium is supposed to be brought into this world. We are liable to do a great deal of damage if we forget our human limitations and concentrate too much on the concrete good we think we should achieve.

Due to our technological concern with efficiency we are liable to overestimate the importance of external achievement. "They also serve who only stand and wait" expresses an attitude toward life which was hard to grasp for Milton, but it has become harder since his days. The experiences of psychosomatic medicine suggest that it is most important that our weaker functions participate in the orientation of our lives. Outstanding achievement through concentration on our specific strengths seems to be a threat to health, and we need to resist the temptation of our culture which promises us rewards for one-sidedness. The balanced use of our functions, the intention and orientation of our lives, those are the long-range tasks of medical hygiene.

So far medicine has treated disease as an evil. Psychosomatic medicine suggests that disease has a positive, spiritual aspect, too. It is an unconscious self-revelation of the limitations of individuality. It suggests that the direction and intent of our common human functions are more valuable than their worldly achievements. In this respect each case of disease must be considered not only an evil to be fought, but also as a reminder of the purpose of life. By this I mean that all human actions and efforts aim toward something which transcends achievement in this world. It may be better that a patient die earlier, reconciled to the meaning of his experience through disease, than to prolong his physical existence by a few years of anxiety and bewilderment.

FOOTNOTE

1. This chapter is adapted by the author from a lecture at the Adelynrood Conference on Theology in Action.

Becoming a Person

*If We Can Provide a Certain Type of
Relationship, the Other Person Will
Discover Within Himself the Capacity
to Use That Relationship for Growth
and Change, and Personal
Development Will Occur* [1]

To be faced by a troubled, conflicted person
who is seeking and expecting help, has always constituted a great challenge to me. Do I have the knowledge, the resources, the psychological strength, the
skill—do I have whatever it takes to be of help to such
an individual?

For more than twenty-five years I have been trying
to meet this kind of challenge. It has caused me to
draw upon every element of my professional background: the rigorous methods of personality measurement which I first learned at Teachers College, Columbia; the Freudian psychoanalytic insights and

methods of the Institute for Child Guidance where I worked as intern; the continuing developments in the field of clinical psychology, with which I have been closely associated; the briefer exposure to the work of Otto Rank, the methods of psychiatric social work, and other contacts too numerous to mention. But most of all it has meant a continual learning from my own experience and that of my colleagues at the Counseling Center as we have endeavored to discover for ourselves effective means of working with people in distress. Gradually I have developed a way of working with people in distress which grows out of that experience, and which can be tested, refined, and reshaped by further experience and research.

One brief way of describing the change which has taken place in me is to say that in my early professional years I was asking the question: How can I treat, or cure, or change this person? Now I would phrase the question this way: How can I provide a relationship which this person may use for his own personal growth?

It is as I have come to put the question in this second way that I realize that whatever I have learned is applicable to all my human relationships, not just to working with clients with problems. It is for this reason that I feel it is possible that the learnings which have had meaning for me in my experience may have some meaning for you in your experience, since all of us are involved in human relationships.

Perhaps I should start with a negative learning. It has gradually been driven home to me that I cannot be of help to this troubled person by means of any intellectual or training procedure. No approach which relies upon knowledge, upon training, upon the acceptance of something that is *taught*, is of any use. These approaches seem so tempting and direct that I have, in the past, tried a great many of them. It is possible to explain a person to himself, to prescribe steps which should lead him forward, to train him in knowledge about a more satisfying mode of life. But such methods are, in my experience, futile and inconsequential. The most they can accomplish is some temporary change, which soon disappears, leaving the individual more than ever convinced of his inadequacy.

The failure of any such approach through the intellect has forced me to recognize that change appears to come about through *experience in a relationship*. So I am going to try to state very briefly and informally some of the essential hypotheses regarding a helping relationship which have seemed to gain increasing confirmation both from experience and research.

I can state the over-all hypothesis in one sentence, as follows: If I can provide a certain type of relationship, the other person will discover within himself the capacity to use that relationship for growth, and change and personal development will occur.

But what meaning do these terms have? Let me take separately the three major phrases in this sentence and indicate something of the meaning they have for me. What is this certain type of relationship I would like to provide?

I have found that the more I can be genuine in the relationship, the more helpful it will be. This means that I need to be aware of my own feelings, in so far as possible, rather than presenting an outward façade of one attitude, while actually holding another attitude at a deeper or unconscious level. Being genuine also involves the willingness to be and to express, in my words and my behavior, the various feelings and attitudes which exist in me. It is only in this way that the relationship can have *reality*, and reality seems deeply important as a first condition. It is only by providing the genuine reality which is in me, that the other person can successfully seek for the reality in him.

As a second condition, I find that the more acceptance and liking I feel toward this individual, the more I shall be creating a relationship which he can use. By acceptance I mean a warm regard for him as a person of unconditional self-worth—of value no matter what his condition, his behavior, or his feelings. It means a respect and liking for him as a separate person, a willingness for him to possess his own feelings in his own way. It means an acceptance of and regard for his attitudes of the moment, no matter how much they may contradict other attitudes he has held in the past. This acceptance of each fluctuating aspect of this other person makes it for him a relationship of warmth and safety, and the safety of being liked and prized as a person seems a highly important element in a helping relationship.

I also find that the relationship is significant to the extent that I feel a continuing desire to understand—a sensitive empathy with each of the client's feelings and communications as they seem to him at that moment. Acceptance does not mean much until it involves understanding. It is only as I *understand* the feelings and thoughts which seem so horrible to you, or so weak, or so sentimental, or so bizarre—it is only as I see them as you see them, and accept them and you, that you can feel really free to explore all the hidden nooks and frightening crannies of your inner and often buried experience. This *freedom* is an important condition of the relationship. There is implied here a freedom to explore oneself at both conscious and unconscious levels, as rapidly as one can dare to embark on this dangerous quest. There is also a complete freedom from any type of moral or diagnostic evaluation since all evaluations are, I believe, always threatening.

Thus the relationship which I have found helpful is characterized by a sort of transparency on my part, in which my real feelings are evident; by an acceptance of this other person as a separate person with value in his own right; and by a deep empathic understanding which enables me to see his private world through his eyes. When these conditions are achieved, I become a companion to my client, accompanying

him in the frightening search for himself, which he
now feels free to undertake.

I am by no means always able to achieve this kind
of relationship with another, and sometimes, even
when I feel I have achieved it in myself, he may be
too frightened to perceive what is being offered to
him. But I would say that when I hold in myself the
kind of attitudes I have described, and when the other
person can to some degree experience these attitudes,
then I believe that change and constructive personal
development will *invariably* occur—and I include that
word "invariably" only after long and careful consideration.

So much for the relationship. The second phrase in
my over-all hypothesis was that the individual will
discover within himself the capacity to use this relationship for growth. I shall try to indicate something
of the meaning which that phrase has for me. Gradually my experience has forced me to conclude that the
individual has within himself the capacity and the
tendency, latent if not evident, to move forward toward maturity. In a suitable psychological climate
this tendency is released and becomes actual rather
than potential. It is evident in the capacity of the individual to understand those aspects of his life and of
himself which are causing him pain and dissatisfaction,
an understanding which probes beneath his conscious
knowledge of himself into those experiences which he
has hidden from himself because of their threatening

nature. It shows itself in the tendency to reorganize his personality and his relationship to life in ways which are regarded as more mature. Whether one calls it a growth tendency, a drive toward self-actualization, or a forward-moving directional tendency, it is the mainspring of life, and is, in the last analysis, the tendency upon which all psychotherapy depends. It is the urge which is evident in all organic and human life—to expand, extend, become autonomous, develop, mature—the tendency to express and activate all the capacities of the organism, to the extent that such activation enhances the organism or the self. This tendency may become deeply buried under layer after layer of encrusted psychological defenses; it may be hidden behind elaborate façades which deny its existence; but it is my belief that it exists in every individual, and awaits only the proper conditions to be released and expressed.

I have attempted to describe the relationship which is basic to constructive personality change. I have tried to put into words the type of capacity which the individual brings to such a relationship. The third phase of my general statement was that change and personal development would occur. It is my hypothesis that in such a relationship the individual will reorganize himself at both the conscious and deeper levels of his personality in such a manner as to cope with life more constructively, more intelligently, and in a more socialized as well as a more satisfying way.

Here I can depart from speculation and bring in the steadily increasing body of solid research knowledge which is accumulating. We know now that individuals who live in such a relationship even for a relatively limited number of hours show profound and significant changes in personality, attitudes, and behavior, changes that do not occur in matched control groups. In such a relationship the individual becomes more integrated, more effective. He shows fewer of the characteristics which are usually termed neurotic or psychotic, and more of the healthy, well-functioning person. He changes his perception of himself, becoming more realistic in his views of self. He becomes more like the person he wishes to be. He values himself more highly. He is more self-confident and self-directing. He has a better understanding of himself, becomes more open to his experience, denies or represses less of his experience. He becomes more accepting in his attitudes toward others, seeing others as more similar to himself.

In his behavior he shows similar changes. He is less frustrated by stress, and recovers from stress more quickly. He becomes more mature in his everyday behavior as this is observed by friends. He is less defensive, more adaptive, more able to meet situations creatively.

These are some of the changes which we now know come about in individuals who have completed a series of counseling interviews in which the psychological

atmosphere approximates the relationship I have described. Each of the statements made is based upon
objective evidence. Much more research needs to be
done, but there can no longer be any doubt as to the
effectiveness of such a relationship in producing personality change.

To me, the exciting thing about these research findings is not simply the fact that they prove the efficacy
of one form of psychotherapy, though that is by no
means unimportant. The excitement comes from the
fact that these findings justify an even broader hypothesis regarding all human relationships. There
seems every reason to suppose that the therapeutic
relationship is only one instance of interpersonal relations, and the same lawfulness governs all such relationships. Thus it seems reasonable to hypothesize that
if the parent creates with his child a psychological
climate such as we have described, then the child will
become more self-directing, socialized, and mature.
To the extent that the teacher creates such a relationship with his class, the student will become a self-initi-
ated learner, more original, more self-disciplined, less
anxious, and other-directed. If the administrator, or
military or industrial leader, creates such a climate
within his organization, then his staff will become
more self-responsible, more creative, better able to
adapt to new problems, more basically co-operative.
It appears possible to me that we are seeing the emergence of a new field of human relationships, in which

we may specify that if certain attitudinal conditions exist, then certain definable changes will occur.

Let me conclude by returning to a personal statement. I have tried to share with you something of what I have learned in trying to be of help to troubled, unhappy, maladjusted individuals. I have formulated the hypothesis which has gradually come to have meaning for me—not only in my relationship to clients in distress, but in all my human relationships. I have indicated that such research knowledge as we have supports this hypothesis, but that there is much more investigation needed. I should like now to pull together into one statement the conditions of this general hypothesis and the effects which are specified.

If I can create a relationship characterized on my part:

by a genuineness and transparency, in which I am my real feelings;

by a warm acceptance of and liking for the other person as a separate individual;

by a sensitive ability to see his world and himself as he sees them;

Then the other individual in the relationship:

will experience and understand aspects of himself which previously he has repressed;

will find himself becoming better integrated, more able to function effectively;

will become more similar to the person he would like to be;

will be more self-directing and self-confident;

will become more of a person, more unique, and more self-expressive;

will be able to cope with the problems of life more adequately and more comfortably.

I believe that this statement holds whether I am speaking of my relationship with a client, with a group of students or staff members, with my family or children. It seems to me that we have here a general hypothesis which offers exciting possibilities for the development of creative, adaptive, inner-directed persons.

FOOTNOTE

1. This chapter represents a lecture by Dr. Rogers given at the Symposium on Emotional Development at Oberlin College. Reprinted by permission.

RELIGION AND PSYCHIATRY

Freud, Psychoanalysis, and Religion

Freud's Basic Beliefs Require Incorporation in
Any Philosophy or Theology That Is to Be
Relevant to the Best Knowledge and Insight
That Man Has into Himself and
His Universe

PSYCHOANALYSIS and religion are not co-ordinate terms. Psychoanalysis is a particular kind of therapeutic process, a particular set of principles (however changing) derived from experience with that process, and a movement of thought initiated by Sigmund Freud. There are and have been differences of conviction about when a therapeutic process, a body of knowledge, or a movement of thought move so far away from Freud that they no longer are to be regarded as psychoanalysis. Freud himself held that, as a body of knowledge, psychoanalysis was a part of general psychology rather than of medicine, and that the

71

crucial matter in the training of the therapist was training in psychoanalysis itself. Other psychoanalysts have disagreed with him. But whatever the legitimate variations in definitions of psychoanalysis, it is always seen as a therapy, a body of knowledge, and a movement of thought initiated by Freud.

No definition of religion ever given would make it wholly co-ordinate with psychoanalysis. Yet there are important co-ordinate points. Religion, in its intention, is always a therapeutic process, in that it attempts to help, to heal, or to save its adherents. It is never seen without certain principles upon which the healing or saving are assumed to rest. And it is always, in some sense, a basic visible movement in history. But all of these points together do not make a definition of religion. The healing and saving process, however it be conceived, is set in a context of following the will of God, and is entered into because it is the will of God, that is, the context in which the process is pursued is essential to understanding its meaning. The principles also, although they deal with man's salvation, can be understood only if seen in the context of man's salvation and healing as being God's will.

Finally, religion is always embodied in a church, consisting of all members and not merely professional practitioners. In all highly developed religions, a distinction of some kind is made between the actual church or movement, and the real or true church. The actual church is always imperfect; the true church is the fellowship of man with him and one another that God wills. Despite the important co-ordinate points between psychoanalysis and religion, therefore, they are not wholly co-ordinate terms. Psychoanalysis is not a complete world view or philosophy of life, a comprehensive fellowship of those who believe in its principles, nor a church actual or invisible.[1] Religion is, or so professes to be. Keeping these distinctions in mind should aid our discussion.

Except for a few persons of firm faith and long perspective, like Oskar Pfister, a Swiss minister who became one of Freud's early colleagues, most religious leaders at first reacted against Freud and psychoanalysis.[2] Some concluded naïvely and incorrectly that he was an advocate of sexual libertinism. Others, with a bit more justice, thought him at best suspicious of any conventional moralities. A good many, joined by philosophers and social scientists, criticized Freud for setting the philosophy of his work within what they regarded as a nineteenth century context, a point which few even among psychoanalysts today would question. But what most disturbed religious leaders about Freud was his direct statements concerning religion. In the title of one well-known book, he called it "illusion," where illusion was understood as that which can neither be proved nor disproved.[3] But the key conception he used in considering religion was not illusion but wishful thinking. Even though the allegations of religion may not be capable of disproof, their truth is inherently improbable because they so obviously correspond with the nature of infantile wish thinking.

His key statement about religion, repeated and stated in different ways in several of his writings, may be summarized as follows.[4] First, religion "gives men information about the source and origin of the universe." Second, it "assures them of protection and final happiness amid the changing vicissitudes of life." Third, it "guides their thoughts and actions by means of precepts which are backed by the whole force of its authority." These claims, Freud implied, are preposterous because they have no verifiable method with which to back them up. If we want to find out how the universe developed, and how its processes began, we study what we can see, and draw inferences that could account for what we see. If we want protection from life's slings and arrows, let us study that we may build better, within and without, to give ourselves strength against them. And if we want to find out what thoughts and actions will most benefit man, let us observe which ones do and which do not.

But religion, as Freud understood it, wanted no truck with such studies. It felt it had the answers. In believing it knew all that was necessary about the source and origin of the universe, it rested on the illusion of pseudo-knowledge. In being convinced of possessing a cosmic insurance policy, it rested on the illusion of pseudo-safety. And knowing just what men should and should not do, it appealed to authoritarian ethics divorced from actual observation. In all three, it was the lack of relevant method that outraged Freud. Why, Freud asked, should anyone be tempted to such inherently improbable ideas except by the weight of unexamined infantile needs? Thus, the root of religious ideas is wishful thinking.[5]

From a sophisticated point of view, it is of course not difficult to show that what high religions like Christianity and Judaism mean, and what Freud referred to, are not the same things. Freud's understandings, it can be contended, are distortions or literalizations that destroy the basic meanings. Belief that God created the universe is not co-ordinate with a view about the stages in its development derived, for example, from sciences like geology or paleontology. The first is an "existential" kind of statement, is to be grasped "mythologically" or "analogically" rather than literally. So with the belief in "protection and final happiness. . . ." If taken literally in insurance policy terms, then this is nonsense as Job found out. But if taken in a larger and more metaphorical sense, then it is not ridiculous at all. If the precepts for man's conduct are literally unexaminable, then Freud's charge would be correct. But it is precisely the religious prophets who have most inveighed against any traditional and unexamined morality. So it can be argued, with little trouble, that Freud made religious beliefs

and religious methods ridiculous when he literalized
them.

But a still more sophisticated view (like that held by
nearly all the great religious leaders of past and present) cannot dispose of Freud's critique so easily. A lot
of religious people (as Freud noted) thought that Dar-
win's theories of evolution and natural selection
threatened their religion, just as others before them
had thought Galileo's theory (against the geocentric
nature of the physical universe) threatened theirs.
There is and always has been, in every religion, a
powerful tendency to literalize a basic insight (or
revelation). When this happens, the prophets have
seen, it becomes an idolatry, setting up a false God
and a false revelation instead of the true God and the
true revelation. So Freud, even though he attacks these
literalizations and distortions of genuine religious insight, can by no means be considered wholly wrong.
In attacking what he attacks, every religious person
with an ounce of prophetism in him will rejoice. We
can never come near the true God unless the false gods
are done away. The breaker of false images is a serv-
ant of the true God, whether he knows it or not.
True, we can get along with him much better if he
makes it clear that what he is breaking is idols. Where,
as in Freud, he fails to do this, he may be misunderstood precisely by those in whose anti-idolatrous cause
he is serving.

In spite of his negative feelings about religion as he understood it, one of the astonishing things about Freud is how much attention he gave to it. Freud began as a medical practitioner; but with the discovery of the psychoanalytic method, it was at once clear to him that the implications went far beyond individual therapy of the neuroses. In a small way, he tried his hand at various areas of implication; he wrote a couple of biographies of famous persons, did a little on art and mythology, made a nod to education, and dealt seriously though briefly with the origin and the destiny of human culture. But his dealing with all these together does not stack up in interest, or even in quantity, with the attention he gave religion. Nor was this, as some observers have wrongly implied, mostly a matter of his declining years when any great man is permitted a few foibles.

He began with a serious article on the similarity between religious behavior and the behavior of "obsessive" patients in 1907.[6] In *Totem and Taboo* (1912), dealing with the origins of society itself, he found himself saying, in effect, that social origins were religious origins.[7] The later books, *The Future of an Illusion* (1925)[8] and *Moses and Monotheism* (1938),[9] deal entirely with religion. *Civilization and Its Discontents* (1930) deals with human culture mainly by way of religion.[10] There are a number of articles in between. Accused by some (who had learned from psychoanalysis that great interest in a subject means something

even when one is consciously against it) of swinging
toward religion, Freud took occasion to deny this in
his *New Introductory Lectures*.[11] His position never
wavered; but he gave more published attention to religion than to anything else except the theory and
practice of psychoanalysis as a therapy.

There seems no good reason to seek far-fetched ex-
planations for this interest. He believed, quite simply,
that religion was the sole possible competitor of science.[12] It was, therefore, the one social force that, because of the hold it could take on people preventing
the search for new truth, might hold back or arrest
man's growing understanding of the universe and of
himself. Art could go its own way though profiting
from the findings of science. Education would be illu-
mined by science. All the functions of culture would
in some way accommodate themselves to these findings, except religion. Thus to Freud religion was the
devil—fascinating, powerful, irrational, the real enemy
against whom only truth might prevail. But it seemed
best to give the devil his due in terms of serious attention.

In the previous section we have considered what
could be called Freud's "critical theology," his battle
against the idolatries of religion. We turn now to what
will be called his "*constructive theology*." Freud
would surely have been horrified by such terms. But
we have already demonstrated that his battle against

distortions and literalizings of religious insight performed a useful theological function. It will now be asserted that what Freud stood *for*, as well as what he stood *against*, also performs useful functions from the theological point of view. In these constructive convictions, Freud was attempting to draw from the observations he had made. He was not thinking of religion or of a constructive theology.

We shall first present five propositions, in our terms rather than Freud's, which can be supported by Freud's writings and his point of view. These were for him basic assertions, generalizations on which his work and thought rested. We present them, so far as possible, in a kind of neutral language that is neither Freud's own nor yet that of traditional theologies.

1. *Actual life can be understood only in terms of its dynamic or driving forces. These forces undercut clear awareness, and therefore have to do with needs, with values, with relationships.*[13] All this follows from the discovery to which Freud gave the name of the "unconscious." If all motivations were clearly conscious, we should not need to assert the dynamic or energetic character of psychic processes. We could really decide for the mashed potatoes or the waistline. But the assertion is necessary because the deciders (regardless of which way they have decided) have denied the nature of the conflict, while psychoanalysis has revealed that nature. There is force (and therefore revelatory meaning) in even the simplest acts and decisions.

Life has depth not always apparent. The resort to conscious clarity may only conceal the real issues, unless the relevant factors are brought to awareness. But if all this is so, then the values of life (that which will meet this or that want or need, of the person or some aspect of him) determine life's decisions, for good or for ill, whether he knows it (in his head) or not. Since so much of these values, wants, and assumed needs have come to one through human relationships, there is a sense in which the relationships (present or recapitulated from the past) govern value choices. Man's psychic life is not flat and superficial; it is not rational in any easy or simple sense. Instead, it is deep, energetic, in conflict, full of self-deception about values, needs, and wants. It is partly irrational though not incapable of becoming genuinely rational as the elements of any conflict are brought together on the same plane and can there fight out genuine value decisions.

2. *The supreme value is truth.*[14] *The great evil is deflection from truth. Truth must be approached directly as well as indirectly, and evil must be fought directly as well as indirectly.* Allegiance to truth is a move toward self-transcendence, a constant reminder against the pull of one's subjectivities. Though he slay me (although the universe may not be concerned to satisfy what seem to be my wants), yet will I trust him (there is something here which must be respected and which it is my minimal job to try to discover). When one voices commitment to truth, he is talking direction-

ally. Part of the truth is unknown, yet to be discovered. It is not dedication to something wholly known, but to something partly known whose unknown reaches command as much as do those that are known. Anything that interferes with the allegiance to truth, and with the quest for further truth, is evil. Thus, he who is unconcerned for the truth is no worse than he who believes he has the truth when he has not. Indeed, the worshiper of idols is worse than he who worships not at all. And how do we move toward truth? We may do so indirectly, as in the revelations of art, of literature, of mythology, and many other human creations, for these enlighten as well as entertain. Yet there can be no substitute for direct attack upon things so that literal truth may be discovered (science). The same is true of the attack upon evil, which may at times be indirect but which must also be direct.

3. *Human freedom comes only through growing awareness of determinism. The degree of such awareness is what decides whether biology and culture shall be in opposition or find some tolerable accommodation.*[15] It was Freud who pointed out that such things as dreams and slips of the tongue, often considered meaningless, are full of revelatory meaning concerning the hidden or nonobvious aspects of personality. Through such observations he reached a point of a "practical determinism," that no bit of behavior is merely arbitrary or capricious. But the understanding of such processes in oneself, Freud saw through the

psychoanalytic procedure itself, means that one is no longer blindly in their grip. Thus freedom in a qualified and practical sense results only through the awareness of one's particular determinisms. This is peculiarly important for the relation between biology and culture, for what Freud called the relation of Id to Super-Ego, for the kind of accommodation or opposition that exists between impulse and social demand. To recognize consciously the nature of these forces is not to make decision unnecessary, but it is to have the battle of values carried on in the open.

4. *The understanding of human life is incomplete without sequential developmental understanding. The principal enemy of such understanding is clinging to old patterns and forms now irrelevant.*[16] Freud shocked the world when he talked about such things as "infantile sexuality," the "Oedipus complex," or "penis-envy." Whether or not one accepts the reality of these in the literal sense in which they were first asserted, another order of reality lies beneath them all, namely, that human development proceeds through a sequence of stages not all the aspects of which are obvious and some aspects of which society has attempted to deny to awareness. If this is true, then learning what the sequential stages are is essential to understanding the actual processes of development. Psychoanalysis disclosed that there are severe resistances to such learning about oneself. The "psychic economy" is thereby disturbed. Far from discovering that people proceed ra-

tionally toward their own best interests, there is a "repetition compulsion," a kind of momentum in the patterns of psychic life, that often makes people act directly against their own best interests. For men to find themselves, therefore, some neutralizing of this force of psychic momentum becomes necessary.

5. *Neither conscience, impulse, nor reason can give adequate clues to what is the good for man. But if brought together into the right relationship, such clues may appear.*[17] Most of conscience, in Freud's view, is the turned-inward edicts and prohibitions taught one by social forces (*via* parents) in early life. It tends, therefore, to be blind, and an unreliable guide. Impulse, to Freud, must find expression, but has no machinery for ascertaining the channel through which it may be expressed without social retribution. Reason, as an affair of the head not comprehending the unconscious, is plainly unreliable since it has access to only some aspects of the personality. But if reason is made, through a process like psychoanalytic therapy, to have access to all the contents of the unconscious, including those of impulse and conscience, then man may be able to see what is the good for him and to follow it. There is no guarantee that he shall do so, however great his insight; for social forces may be arrayed against him. Nothing will protect him from the open struggle in deciding for and against values. But if this road is difficult and unsure, there is no other that can stand a chance of helping him discover and follow his good.[18]

Assuming that these statements are justified conclusions from Freud, then it should be further noted that they all hang together. They are not a set of discrete points, of which we may take some and let the others go. Each presupposes all the others. If we accept what Freud meant by the "unconscious," then we must also believe in freedom coming only through awareness of determinism, in sequential developmental understanding, and the rest. This is another way of saying that Freud was more systematic in his thinking than he may have supposed.[19] For the system simply deals with the actualities of relationship as he understood them, and is not something imposed from an external logical pattern. It is not an illogical pattern; but the content with which the logic operates includes factors arising from the discovery of the "unconscious" not contained in previous logical systems.

Someone may well ask what is theological about these propositions. Admittedly, they do not sound theological in any traditional sense. But each of them, and all of them together, try to deal with man as he actually is in relation to man as he may become provided he is alert to certain things in the nature of reality. They do not talk of God but of truth. But they set forth conditions regarded as indispensable to man's movement toward truth and good. The originality of Freud's own contributions stems from his understanding of the "unconscious," and therefore the nature of freedom, of conscience, of reason, of impulse, of development, and of values, in human things.

One may ask further why this is linked in any way with theology. Granted that there is a kind of philosophy of life implied in the propositions, is that not sufficient? Is not a theology something different? Of course, the answer depends upon one's view of the relationship between philosophy and theology. In the sense that these convictions of Freud were arrived at by him as an individual, in an attempt to account for phenomena as he observed them, they are certainly a philosophy. But if the view he held that a theology always contains a philosophy, that it is in a tradition and a movement, that it is passionately concerned and not just detached, then one could say that in some measure Freud's propositions approach a theological character. To suggest that they are like theology would be sufficient for our purposes. What is most important to recognize is that they perform a theological function, a linking together of basic concerns in a way regarded (so far as the propositions go) as normative for human beings.

It is hardly necessary to state that what we have called "Freud's theology" is not a complete theology. To many aspects of the question about man's origin, meaning, and destiny Freud did not address himself at all. Our assertion is that Freud did set forth a constructive philosophy of life in such a way that it could form part of a constructive theology.

It would seem difficult to one not an obscurantist to hold a constructive theology relevant to our day that would not include Freud's five points. Consider briefly what would happen if each of them in turn should be denied.

Suppose, first, that we should assert that actual life could be understood in static and surface terms. We should then be surface rationalists, denying the depth dimensions of life to which all our religious traditions give testimony.

Or suppose, second, that we should make the search for truth something of merely secondary merit. If truth were not believed to have its own integrity, we should turn into opportunists of the fascist type, using knowledge only as the instrument of arbitrary will, whether in political or other matters. Third, suppose that we held that human freedom has nothing to do with the awareness of the ways in which we have been determined. We should then become irresponsible voluntarists, confusing freedom with arbitrariness, and unaware of our own individual and collective histories.

If we held, fourth, that sequential developmental understanding is not necessary, then we should become evaluators of a moralistic kind, having no comprehension of how any human phenomenon has actually become as it is. And we should have no genuine knowledge of human motivation. Finally, if we plunked for conscience, or impulse, or reason, as the keys to man's salvation, we should become blind moralists, or irresponsible libertines, or cold rationalists.

Freud's basic beliefs, therefore, require incorporation in any philosophy or theology that is to be relevant to the best knowledge and insight that man has into himself and his universe.

Having gone so far with Freud, perhaps we should go one step further, and ask what would probably have been his response to this analysis? It has already been suggested that he would have approved the propositions, although perhaps requesting a restatement of them . . . Would he have acknowledged them as making a contribution to a constructive theology? Perhaps he would have been, temporarily, amused. He would probably have said, then, that anything promoting these points is good, but that religion does not do so. If we had averred that many theologians would accept the points and regard them as important, he would have implied that religion is a social force not because of the theologians' beliefs but because of the blind commitment of the people.[20] He might have accused the theologians of neutralizing the force of his points by associating them with others he would regard as absurd; but in any event, he would have wondered why the theologians want to put up an "intellectual front" when their understandings do not affect the blind belief and loyalty of the masses of the people.

Support for this interpretation of Freud's probable response is drawn from a letter he wrote to John G.

Greene, a Unitarian minister, who had written Freud
of some religious movements in the United States and
asking whether these did not differ from the religion
Freud had analyzed. Freud replied, in effect, that the
values Greene described, in humanitarian terms, were
certainly worth seeking; but why did so many intelligent people in the United States have to waste so
much of their energy on doing this within a religious
framework?

Even if we do not take into account the movements
away from Freudian psychoanalysis as in Adler, Jung,
or Rank, but confine ourselves to those that have remained affiliated with psychoanalytic societies, *there
have been considerable changes in psychoanalytic theory as well as practice*. Freud himself began the change
process. But certain kinds of changes which were actually taking place were not much spoken of until after
Freud's death in the late nineteen thirties.

The changes in theory, with which we are here concerned, could be legitimately described in various
ways. The increasing attention to social and cultural
factors and forces, the change in the understanding of
feminine psychology, and an explicit concern for
values and ethics might be noted.

A more general way to see the changes in psychoanalytic theory is by analogy to processes that have
taken place again and again in religious history, usually now called "mythologizing" and "demythologiz-

ing." As an illustration, we may look to the Oedipus complex. Freud discovered initially, in dealing with his adult patients, evidence that suggested that when they had been children, they had had desires to possess the parent of the opposite sex and to destroy the parent of the same sex. The phenomenon itself, more complicated than this simple statement, he called the Oedipus complex. At first he understood it in more or less literal terms. Later there came a period of deliteralizing this concept. Then, in a person like Erich Fromm, there was a conscious "mythologizing" of it—indicating that it pointed to a basic truth but that this real truth was lost if stated literally. Others are now trying to "demythologize" the concept—to winnow out what is literally true from what is symbolically true. There tends now to be a tension between the mythologizers and the demythologizers.

In religion this tension has had a long history. Many of us believe it must be preserved, that any attempt to become entirely symbolic or entirely literal is bound to lose significant facets of the truth. The tension was well illustrated in the discussions on the main theme of a recent Assembly of the World Council of Churches, concerning "The Christian Hope." To think in merely symbolic fashion of the end of human history proved inadequate; and plainly, to think in merely literal fashion of such an end was not helpful. The partly successful efforts of the Assembly to keep these two modes of thought in tension were, to be sure, difficult for the uninitiated to comprehend. But religion is not the sole field of human thought where such a continuing tension is necessary to render the situation accurately.

It would seem essential for psychoanalytic thought to return again and again to Freud; for even when something that he saw literally may have to be rejected, it may point to something even more important when grasped symbolically, as in his theory of character types. Yet it would seem equally important to recognize the new discoveries and modes of thought that move beyond Freud. So psychoanalysis, to continue its own theoretical progress, must move constantly between observation and tradition, between trying new concepts and returning to a more profound interpretation of old ones, maintaining a tension between mythologizing and demythologizing. Psychoanalytic theory is a product both of science and of philosophy. The more clearly this is understood, the more psychoanalytic thought will be aware of its similarities to religious and theological thought, at least in terms of method.

The recent movements in psychoanalytic thought make it much easier for the theologian to grasp than before. It must now touch upon sociology, upon anthropology, upon economics, and upon ethics in a way that was not necessary at first. There is a decreasing temptation to a mere positivism, and a biologism has practically died in psychoanalytic thought at the same time better attention is being given to biology. All these developments make it easier for the theologian to learn from psychoanalysis, and to see it as an ally rather than as the enemy of all sound religion.

We may now ask briefly *what, if any, are the most basic contributions that psychoanalysis has made possible in relation to religious understanding?* Three will be mentioned.

First, when the religious quest is rightly understood, psychoanalysis has given new grounds for declaring its legitimacy and importance in human life. Fromm's "frame of orientation and devotion" can certainly not be reduced to the projection of father images. The quest for the ground of being which is also the ground of one's own being (and which Jews and Christians believe to have revealed itself in certain ways in actual historical events) is not in itself a pathological search. If man does not so seek, he is truncating the development of an essential dimension of his own being.

Second, psychoanalysis has provided valuable new insights for understanding the distortions of the religious quest. People may and often do believe in a god who is a projection of father images, in a Christ or Mary who is a magic helper, in a holy spirit reputed to relieve one of personal responsibility. The psychic processes by which such distortions occur need to be known. Only so can these idolatries be exposed in whatever form they appear.

Third, psychoanalysis has made available tools that can be used for the actual enrichment of religious doctrine itself. For example, Luther's doctrine of "justification by faith alone" seems almost incomprehensible to modern ears. And yet psychoanalysis has demonstrated that the release of therapy does not arise directly out of effort, however hard or compulsive, but out of relaxation, acceptance, a kind of surrender to life as it really is. This is rediscovery, but it can also help to explain some aspects of the process on which Luther was (properly enough for his time) unclear. In this sense psychoanalysis is a potentially constructive agent, and not merely analytic.

On the other side, there are some indications that *theology is beginning to make a significant impact upon psychoanalytic thought*, even though the source is not always acknowledged. We shall comment briefly on three such contributions.

First, psychoanalysis has moved beyond its initial complete identification with science, and increasingly recognizes its roots as being existential as well as scientific. This means no lessening of its scientific concern, but a broadening of its understanding of the meaning of science; and a further recognition that, in the life and death issues always posed by actual therapy, one always transcends whatever he clearly knows.

Second, psychoanalysis is increasingly impressed

vith interpersonal relationships, the social fabric, that
nen are, in Christian terms "members one of another."

Third, psychoanalysis is beginning to recognize that,
n its suspicion of legalism, moralism, and rationalism,
ts powerful ally is religion. It was not the first oppo-
ient of these trends, although it has forged new
veapons for the battle.

To speak in generally positive terms of the relation-
hip, actual and potential, between psychoanalysis and
eligion, runs the risk of suggesting that the issues and
ensions are of secondary significance. Such issues and
ensions exist, and many will continue to exist despite
ny efforts made to relieve them. As we suggested at
he beginning, these two are not coterminous, and a
nisunderstanding of the fact produces tensions. Be-
ides, what we have said about religion in general must
lways be qualified in relation to each religion in par-
icular; and perhaps something similar on a smaller
cale must be said of groups of psychoanalysts.

But these are no longer enemies who cannot even
neet at the conference table. Discussion can be held.
There is enough recognition of mutual interest to war-
ant conversation about that interest. And there is
ufficient concern to find agreement, and to clarify dis-
greement, to impel such discussion. Psychoanalytic
hought is not a fixed and final system, and there is in-
reasing recognition of this fact. And neither is re-
igion and religious understanding; for religion (unlike

God) is a human enterprise subject to all the fallibi-
lities that flesh is heir to. Each may help the other to
understand its distortions. Each may help to legitima-
tize the quest. And each may find its theory more
relevant to the other than it had at first supposed. Even
where one cannot agree, he may be richer.

FOOTNOTES

1. Freud wrote, "Psycho-analysis is not, in my opinion, in
a position to create a *Weltanschauung* of its own . . . it makes
no claim to being comprehensive or to constituting a system."
New Introductory Lectures on Psychoanalysis (Norton
1933) p. 248. Indeed, "Psychoanalysis has never claimed to
provide a complete theory of human mentality as a
whole . . ." *Collected Papers, I* (Hogarth, 1924), p. 378.

2. For a representative comment on Pfister by Freud, see
An Autobiographical Study (Norton, 1935), p. 133.

3. *The Future of an Illusion* (Liveright, 1928).

4. *New Introductory Lectures on Psychoanalysis,* pp.
220-221.

5. "The whole thing is so patently infantile, so incongru-
ous with reality, that to one whose attitude to humanity is
friendly it is painful to think that the great majority of
mortals will never be able to rise above this view of life."
Civilization and Its Discontents (Hogarth, 1930), p. 23.

6. "Obsessive Acts and Religious Practices," *Collected
Papers, II* (Hogarth, 1924), pp. 25-35.

7. "Totem and Taboo," *The Basic Writings of Sigmund
Freud* (Modern Library, 1938), pp. 807-930.

8. (Liveright, 1928).

9. (Knopf, 1938).

10. (Hogarth, 1930).

11. (Norton, 1933), p. 78.

12. "Of the three forces which can dispute the position
of science, religion alone is a really serious enemy." *Ibid.*
p. 219.

13. For the simplest descriptions by Freud of the dynamic character of psychic life, see *An Autobiographical Study*, pp. 52ff., and *A General Introduction to Psycho-Analysis* (Liveright, 1935), e.g., "Our purpose is not merely to describe and classify the phenomena, but to conceive them as brought about by the play of forces in the mind, as expressions of tendencies striving towards a goal, which work together or against one another. We are endeavouring to attain a dynamic conception of mental phenomena." *Ibid.*, p. 60. Psychoanalysis, Freud also wrote, has led to "a fresh scale of values in scientific thought." *An Autobiographical Study*, p. 81. On the conception of need, "A better term for a stimulus of instinctual origin is a 'need'; that which does away with this need is 'satisfaction.'" *Collected Papers, IV* (Hogarth, 1925), p. 62. Freud's over-all view is seen in a postscript written in 1938, "I perceived ever more clearly that the events of human history, the interactions between human nature, cultural development and the precipitates of primaeval experiences (the most prominent example of which is religion) are no more than a reflection of the dynamic conflicts between the ego, the id, and the super-ego, which psychoanalysis studies in the individual—are the very same processes repeated upon a wider stage." *An Autobiographical Study*, p. 138.

14. One of the most striking statements about truth is this ". . . our god *logos* is not perhaps a very powerful one; he may only fulfill a small part of what his forerunners have promised." *The Future of an Illusion*, p. 95. The forerunners referred to are chiefly religion. Again, ". . . truth cannot be tolerant and cannot admit compromise or limitations . . ." *New Introductory Lectures*, p. 219. "Our object is that of all scientific endeavour—namely, to achieve an understanding of the phenomena, to establish a connection between them, and, in the last resort, wherever it is possible to increase our power over them." *A General Introduction to Psycho-Analysis*, p. 90. Further proof that truth to Freud was not static is found in this, "The day will come, where and when we know not, when every little piece of knowledge will be converted into power, and into therapeutic power." *Ibid.*, p. 227. Not only is truth to be sought and cherished in gen-

eral but also in the individual psychic life. "As a rule it is
soon apparent that by accepting a neurosis the ego has made
a bad bargain. It has paid too heavily for the solution of the
conflict; the sufferings entailed by the symptoms are perhaps
as bad as those of the conflict they replace, and they may
quite probably be very much worse." *Ibid.*, p. 334. Distortion, we might say, does not pay. This makes it perhaps a
bit easier to pursue truth. But truth would have to be pursued in any event.

15. The subjective feeling of freedom is unjustified, Freud
felt. He wrote that "the deeply rooted belief in psychic
freedom and choice . . . must give ground before the claims
of a determinism which governs even mental life." *A General Introduction to Psycho-Analysis*, p. 95. Indeed, the utility
of "free association" in psychoanalysis is precisely because
"free association is not really free" in the sense of jumping
out of a deterministic chain. *An Autobiographical Study*, p.
76. But in contrast to this illusion of freedom, there is something that can be called real freedom, and it is the task of
psychoanalysis to foster this. ". . . analysis does not set out
to abolish the possibility of morbid reactions, but to give
the patient's ego *freedom* to choose one way or the other."
The Ego and the Id (Hogarth, 1927), p. 72, note 1. Psychoanalysis might be described as a process that helps its patients
move toward genuine freedom, for their problem is of un-
freedom. Patients "give the impression that they are '*fixed*'
to a particular point in their past, that they do not know how
to release themselves from it, and are consequently alienated
from both present and future." *A General Introduction to
Psycho-Analysis*, p. 242. As to the accommodation of what
has here been called biology and culture, both have significant claims. As to the former, "Thus the cry for freedom is
directed either against particular forms or demands of culture or else against culture itself." *Civilization and Its Discontents*, p. 60. As to the latter, "Civilized man has exchanged
some part of his chances of happiness for a measure of
security. " *Ibid.*, p. 92. Since Freud was so often accused of
being anticultural in general and antimoral in particular, the
following rather early statement is instructive, ". . . anyone
who has successfully undergone the training of learning and

recognizing the truth about himself is henceforth strengthened against the dangers of immorality, even if his standard
of morality should in some respect deviate from the common
one." *A General Introduction to Psycho-Analysis*, p. 377.
It was not morality, nor a sensitivity to culture, that Freud
found devastating in his patients, but a legalistic morality of
conformity containing understanding neither of oneself nor
of culture.

16. Freud's discussion of what is here called "sequential
developmental understanding" began with the stages of sexual development in early childhood, and was later generalized
to throw light on character as such. Freud himself never
made a comprehensive or general attempt to describe all or
most of the factors involved in the sequence, but put his own
attention only on those factors he felt had been overlooked.
Yet the lead he gave has been invaluable to later investigators
especially of child development. Freud has often been called
a hedonist; and indeed many of his statements would support
such a view if not read in the context of his thought as a
whole. But one of his most important discoveries was that
people do not, in fact, follow the "pleasure principle." Instead ". . . there really does exist in the mind a compulsion
to repeat which overrides the pleasure principle." *Beyond
the Pleasure Principle* (Liveright, 1950), p. 25. In dealing
with patients Freud found ". . . no lesson has been learnt
from the old experience of these activities having led instead
only to unpleasure. In spite of that they are repeated, under
pressure of compulsion." *Ibid.*, p. 23. The compulsive clinging to old patterns and stages is, therefore, the principal
enemy of psychic progress. And beyond pleasure, for Freud,
is always truth; but he felt there should be no contradiction
here, for "The very nature of reason is a guarantee that it
would not fail to concede to human emotions . . . the position to which they are entitled." *New Introductory Lectures
on Psychoanalysis*, p. 234. That is, in so far as Freud may be
called a hedonist, it is because he felt a seeking for pleasure
or happiness in an effective way was related to the search
for truth and was not in opposition to it. The "repetition
compulsion," on the other hand, was an enemy both to truth
and to happiness.

17. Conscience is regarded by Freud as unreliable. In referring to Kant's famous statement he wrote, "The stars are unquestionably superb, but where conscience is concerned God has been guilty of an uneven and careless piece of work . . ." *New Introductory Lectures on Psychoanalysis* p. 88. Impulse is not enough, for "psychoanalysis is an instrument to enable the ego to push its conquest of the id further still." *The Ego and the Id*, p. 82. And reason, Freud felt, when understood as philosophers generally have done is also unreliable, ". . . the delusions of paranoiacs have an unpalatable external similarity and internal kinship to the systems of our philosophers." *Collected Papers, V* (Hogarth 1950), p. 94. Freud's solution is at times phrased in terms of a reason that respects emotions, e.g., "Our best hope for the future is that the intellect—the scientific spirit, reason—should in time establish a dictatorship over the human mind. The very nature of reason is a guarantee that it would not fail to concede to human emotions . . . the position to which they are entitled." *New Introductory Lectures on Psychoanalysis*, p. 234.

Sometimes Freud writes in terms of the expansion of consciousness, "Without the light shed by the quality of consciousness we should be lost in the darkness of depth psychology." *Ibid.*, p. 99. Cf. *The Ego and the Id*, p. 18. This way of talking about intellect, reason, and consciousness sometimes make it appear that Freud's theory is a new gnosticism, but there is always an important qualification to such a conclusion, e.g., ". . . The necessary condition is that the knowledge must be founded upon an inner change in the patient which can only come about by a mental operation directed to that end." *A General Introduction to Psycho Analysis*, p. 249. Freud stated again and again that the knowledge or insight that could relieve conflicts was, so to speak, preliminary to other tasks of human living and not a substitute for these tasks. ". . . the pathogenic conflict in neurotic must not be confounded with a normal struggle between conflicting impulses all of which are in the same mental field . . . an effective decision can be reached only when they confront each other on the same ground . . . to accomplish this is the sole task of the treatment." *Ibid.*, p. 370

Although Freud concentrated on helping neurotics in the sense suggested above, he was fully aware of the need to apply additional criteria when life as a whole was in view. "It must not be forgotten that there are healthy persons as well as unhealthy ones who are good for nothing in life." *Collected Papers, I*, p. 257. Many such people could not profit from psychoanalysis, because for that ". . . a certain measure of natural intelligence and ethical development may be required . . ." *Ibid.*, p. 270. The following statement of the human psychic predicament by Freud sounds unusually like that of a theologian such as Kierkegaard, ". . . the normal man is not only far more immoral than he believes but also far more moral than he has any idea of . . ." *The Ego and the Id*, p. 75.

It would be fair to say that Freud regarded the good for man as appearing when the ego, as he understood it, assumed genuine control of the elements of psychic life; but this was precisely because only the ego (informed by true reason) could give each element of psychic life its due, bring a tolerable accommodation between biology and culture, move toward freedom, and be guided by truth. "A person only falls ill of a neurosis when the ego loses its capacity to deal in some way or other with the libido." *A General Introduction to Psycho-Analysis*, p. 336. But when put in this way, it is necessary to recall that Freud had a complex notion of the ego, including the point that ". . . not only what is lowest but also what is highest in the ego can be unconscious." *The Ego and the Id*, p. 33. Freud has at times been called an ascetic, at others a libertine, at still others a rationalist. There is more justification for the last than for the others, but this fails to understand how he used the terms "ego," "reason," "intellect," and the like.

18. "No, science is no illusion. But it would be an illusion to suppose that we could get anywhere else what it cannot give us." *The Future of an Illusion*, p. 98.

19. The notion of a "system" seemed to Freud to call for rejection on two related counts. First, a system is thought of as antiscientific and an enemy to truth, because it lays claim to an adequacy and comprehensiveness that the open-minded scientific worker finds unacceptable. Second, a system seems

to be thought of as something externally imposed, thus distorting the various details that make it up. Freud's main complaint against Adler was in relation to system. "The Adlerian theory was from the very beginning a 'system,' which psycho-analysis was very careful to avoid becoming." *Collected Papers, I*, p. 340. Rightly suspicious of a "clear and distinct idea" approach, Freud felt that "clear fundamental concepts and sharply drawn definitions are only possible in the mental sciences in so far as the latter seek to fit a department of facts into the frame of a logical system." *An Autobiographical Study*, p. 110. Pointing to some of his own ideas as "part of a speculative superstructure of psychoanalysis," he stated that "any portion" of this superstructure "can be abandoned or changed without loss or regret the moment its inadequacy has been proved." *Ibid.*, p. 60. What he did not see was that system may mean something different, the kind of thing he himself did in adhering to a very few basic ideas that all his experience and work reinforced, and that were seen in relationship to one another. That system may be limited, and that awareness of its systematic character may be necessary if it is to remain open, he was inclined to disbelieve.

20. "We will now go back to the ordinary man and his religion—the only religion that ought to bear the name." *Civilization and Its Discontents*, p. 24. Freud was merciless against what the philosophers and theologians did to the ordinary man's religion. "Philosophers . . . may even pride themselves on having attained a higher and purer idea of God, although their God is nothing but an insubstantial shadow and no longer the mighty personality of religious doctrine." *The Future of an Illusion*, p. 57.

WALTER M. HORTON

A Psychological Approach to Theology — After 25 Years

Theology and Psychology Deal with Different Dimensions of the Same Deeply Tormented, Divinely Exalted, and Demonically Possessed Creature Known as Man; and Their Findings and Insights Often Check and Corroborate One Another from Different Angles

M Y STUDY of psychology has generally been in a religious context. The reading of William James' *Varieties of Religious Experience* was one of the great religious experiences of my college years. The study of religious education and psychology of religion under George Albert Coe was so important a feature of my theological studies that I remember making the following generalization toward the end of my course at Union Theological Seminary: for a good longitudi-

nal section of the religious phenomenon, read as much
history as you can; for a good cross section of it, so
close to its vital principle that it bleeds when you make
the incision, study *psychology*. Between the two, you
have the principal raw materials for true religious insight, and sound theology.

This conclusion was still firmly fixed in my mind
when I began to teach theology at Oberlin thirty years
ago. I began very early to teach a course in applied
psychology for theological students, and have kept it
up ever since—first with a strongly theological slant
but increasingly with a pastoral slant. From the case
studies of problem parishioners handed in by students
in this course, I have gotten many new insights. Out
of this course grew my first attempt to make an original statement of a full-length theology: *A Psychological Approach to Theology* (1931).

As I look back upon this book, twenty-five years
later, I find that while many of my views have
changed, I still retain the strong conviction that psychology is one of the perennial sources of religious insight, and a psychological approach to theology will
always therefore be one legitimate and necessary approach. It has puzzled me and troubled me that
through the greater part of those twenty-five years
this rich vein of religious insight has not been sys-
tematically worked by theologians. It is only recently
that men like the late Professor David Roberts of
Union Seminary, Professor Albert Outler of S.M.U.

and Paul Tillich have returned to it. (Roberts, *Psychotherapy and a Christian View of Man*; Outler, *Psychotherapy and the Christian Message*; Tillich, *The Courage to Be*.) Perhaps it is worth while to pause and consider the causes of this long neglect and this recent return.

1. *Sociological causes.* The great economic depression had already begun with the Wall Street crash of 1929, shortly before my book was published. Economic distress, mounting political tensions, World War II passing over without a break into cold war, Korean War, and all sorts of "brink of war" situations, have preoccupied the public mind ever since. In the end, those accumulated sociological strains have resulted in what is now called the "age of anxiety," whose psychological issues simply *must* be met; but for some years they served to divert attention from psychology. There was a time when "FDR" could declare, "Private lives are repealed," and it was practically true.

2. *Theological causes.* When my book was written, the liberal theology based on religious experience, which Schleiermacher started in Germany, and Horace Bushnell brought to America, was still influential. For such an experience-centered theology, psychology was an obviously important source. Wobbermin had lately incorporated William James' psychology of religion into this school of thought and referred to the resultant theology as "Schleiermacher-Jamesian." I cited this

as an important precedent for my own attempt at a psychological approach to theology. Since then, however, the "neo-orthodox" trend has transferred the emphasis in theology from psychological experience to historical revelation, where God is met in his "mighty acts" coming from above and beyond human experience.

I have sympathized with this shift myself to a considerable extent. I believe in the uniqueness of the Bible's insight into the divine meaning of once-for-all, unrepeatable events such as Israel's deliverance from Egypt and Babylon, or the crucifixion and triumph of Jesus—events which in spite of their once-for-allness have the power to illuminate the meaning of other events, thousands of years later. A *purely* experience-centered, *purely* psychological approach to theology tended to obscure this supreme source of religious insight; yet there was no need to *exclude* the psychological approach to theology in order to reinstate the idea of historic revelation in its proper place. Tillich, who refuses to make religious experience the main source of his theology, nevertheless recognizes that revelation (for him, the main source) must be *received in experience*—which gives the psychological approach all the character it needs.[1]

In some neo-orthodox theology this point is not grasped; so the authority of the Bible and of traditional theological terms tends to be rigidly asserted, in a way that does not "speak to man's condition." Man's condition, however, can never be safely neglected by theology. Psychological study of man's condition was developing all the time that theology was neglecting it. Neglect only meant that people felt psychology was something wholly apart from theology, and quite opposed to religion—something they were disposed to turn to as religion failed them. What theology's return to psychology now makes us realize is that theology and psychology deal with different dimensions of the same deeply tormented, divinely exalted, and demonically possessed creature known as man; and their findings and insights often check and corroborate one another from different angles.

Roberts, Outler, and Tillich all agree substantially with the position I took twenty-five years ago, that theology and psychology both need to become aware of their own limitations if they are to co-operate effectively. Roberts, for example, warns against "psychologism" which claims "that psychology, by itself, can determine the validity of religious beliefs"—or even (I may add) *do the work of religion by itself*, as I once heard Pierre Janet claim that scientific psychiatry could carry on efficiently that very "cure of souls" which religion had always carried on in a bungling way! On the other hand, Roberts warns against "theologism" which claims, in effect, that Christianity has nothing to learn from secular disciplines—as when "theologians continue to write books about the doctrine of man which ignore or conflict with recent work on psychology and anthropology." [2] These fallacies can be avoided if it is once clearly realized that religion and theology deal with man in his total reaction to the profoundest meanings of Total Reality, while psychology (like all empirical sciences) deals with man from an abstract and specialized point of view.

Hugo Münsterberg (with whom I began to study general psychology as a college freshman, back in 1913–14) said in his opening lecture that a human person can be regarded from either a "purposive" or a "causal" point of view. As my friend with whom I converse, he is primarily a source of meanings and purposes, with whom my own meanings and purposes can enter into conversation. But when something he says or does awakens my psychological curiosity— "how did he get that way?"—I treat him thenceforth as a "case," and subject him to causal explanation until my problem about him is solved and I feel free to treat him again as fully personal and purposive. Martin Buber would say that in this process I pass from I— Thou to I-It, and back again. Clearly, the I-Thou perspective is more ultimately true, but for analysis of particular problems of human behavior, both normal and abnormal, particular aspects of the man need to be studied in abstraction from the whole man.

I tell my theological students that they are not to suppose they have fully understood their problem parishioners when they have simply classified them as cases of a certain type—schizoids, or psychopaths, or normal delinquents, or what-not—but need to try to see how their unique character and circumstances color their problem, whatever it is. Yet I also tell them that they may totally misjudge these persons if they do not study them as cases of a special type, needing to be explained and treated quite differently from those of other types. Christian theology and ethics require them to be *friends* to those people, as persons precious in God's sight; but psychology requires them to show their friendship differently to a normally lonely person seeking "recognition and response," and to a psychopathic person making impossible demands of everyone he buttonholes.

As a beautiful example of the way that theology and psychology can co-operate when they both recognize their limitations, I remember a case described by Fritz Kunkel at a ministerial conference. The case was brought to Kunkel by a pastor who realized that it was beyond his limitations. Here was a man, fundamentally loyal to his family, who periodically went on a general spree of irresponsible dissipation from which he came out miserably ashamed and vowing never to do it again—but presently did. Kunkel found that this man had once wanted to take up an artistic career, but been thwarted by his mother, who thought it no career for a "he-man." Kunkel advised him to take up an artistic hobby of some sort, which immensely released the pressure that drove him periodically to dissipation. But still he was oppressed by guilt, for he found he hated his mother for what she had done to him. At this point, Kunkel and his patient went back to the pastor for a talk on the religious meaning of forgiveness and the theology of Original Sin—which enabled the man to comprehend and accept the tragedy of his mother's real but perverted affection for him. Psychology plus theology healed him more deeply than either could by itself.

Let me try now to restate briefly some of the main theses of a psychological approach to theology, in the light of twenty-five years of further development on both sides.

1. *Both psychology and theology use symbolical language to present their findings, but the symbols are of a different order, and point to the same realities from widely different angles*. Like all scientific symbols, psychology's are abstract and diagrammatic; like artistic and literary symbols, theology's are concrete and suggestive of rich meanings and values. In Streeter's *Reality*, the first type of "representation" is compared to a Baedeker map which a tourist takes to Venice to show him the location of all the points of interest; the second type is compared to a Turner painting of a Venetian sunset, which the same tourist takes with him to open his eyes to glories he might miss. It has become a commonplace of theology in re-

cent years that the truth of the biblical revelation is not of the precisely diagrammatic order—though derived from actual history and so relevant to real life—but much of it is expressed in myths and parables which interpret the drama of God-man relationships in great sweeping strokes, inexact in detail but profoundly true in their main lines. A theology that recognizes this can reconcile biblical revelation with psychological findings about man's fundamental drives, their deviations, and their integrations.

2. *The basis of human life in the fundamental human drives is essentially sound.* Psychology assumes this in its theory of integration and adjustment. John Dewey in *Human Nature and Conduct* says there are three alternative destinies for every drive or impulse: random discharge, repression, and organization. Repression is no way to solve the problem of unorganized, dissipated behavior; any impulse treated as bad in itself and so repressed from consciousness becomes uncontrollable and revenges itself in ways that psychoanalysis has vividly described. When treated as good in itself and organized, the same impulse may help to build strong character. Interestingly enough, Dewey never mentions a fourth possibility, which Oriental mysticism takes quite seriously: to encourage the drive to melt away into that cool detachment and absence of desire which Buddhists call *Nirvana*. Evidently Dewey was more influenced by biblical insights than he consciously recognized; for it is a basic part of

biblical revelation that human nature as God created it is good, like all else that God creates. Moreover, man is represented in the Bible as made in the divine image, capable within limits of creative reorganization of nature ("dominion over the creatures") and even of creative reorganization of his own nature, such as psychology undertakes in the process of "conditioning." Whatever God gives man in creation, whether in nature or in himself, is good raw material only, calling out for creative reconditioning.

3. *Man can be alienated from himself, from his fellows, and from his creative Source in a great variety of ways, all involving a destructive perversion of an essentially good drive. The perversion starts with anxiety, which then leads to loss of faith and various forms of self-protective or despairing behavior.* Psychotherapy classifies human disorders into various types, for purposes of diagnosis and treatment: psychoses, neuroses, crime and delinquency, sex perversion, drug addiction, pre-neurotic maladjustments, and so on. Behind each of these types of disorder it sees a normal drive which has failed to achieve normal organization, and which often cannot be redirected by the person who has it, because of social or mental conflicts that trap him in a vicious circle. Biblical revelation describes this whole complex situation as a state of sin. Theologism thinks it can cover sin-in-general with a blanket formula that will dispose of it (say, by substitutionary atonement) without going carefully

into the varieties of human conditions and problems. I fought against this theologism in my *Psychological Approach*, demanding a specific cure for each specific kind of human ill; but I also fought against the psychologism that treats sin and guilt as pathological illusions; and I regarded the separate forms of human disorder as "symptoms" of a deeper disorder whose roots go to the bottom of universal being, and for which "sin" is the only adequate term.

Recent psychology and theology have done much to fill in the crude sketch I made of the symptoms, cause, and cure of sin. On the psychological side, the "cultural" school of psychoanalysts (notably Karen Horney) have discovered that neuroses are caused by deeper and wider factors than the traumatic experiences of the individual; a competitive society tends to generate a kind of collective neurosis in all its members. If then we ask whether culture is the *ultimate* environment that conditions the neurotic, the way is opened for a still deeper diagnosis. Paul Tillich in *The Courage to Be* insists that the anxiety from which our age suffers is not merely a pathology due to particular contingent causes; its deepest root is *existential anxiety*, inevitable in all cultures for finite creatures like us. Reinhold Niebuhr in *The Nature and Destiny of Man* has shown with deep insight and compassion how existential anxiety (innocent and necessary in itself) leads over into various sorts of sin by way of unbelief, pride, and sensuality. Between Horney's theory of neurosis and the theology of sin in Tillich and Niebuhr, there is a remarkable convergence. Both theories have been deeply influenced by Kierkegaard's studies in "dread" and "despair," which are rich both in psychological insight and in theological vision.

4. *Man begins to be restored to his true nature when he honestly sees and confesses his wrongness in the presence of a love that accepts him just as he is and believes in his better possibilities.* Psychological counseling uses the term "acceptance," while theology speaks of "justification" by faith in forgiving grace and points to essentially the same kind of love as the objective condition for new beginnings in life. In my *Psychological Approach* I pointed to the analogy between "abreaction" in psychoanalysis, "insight" as a turning-point in the cure of young delinquents, and a similar candor about one's own wrongness as the turning point in religious conversion. The love that "accepts" such confessions when they are blurted out is not devoid of all concern for moral distinctions; it often suffers greatly with and for the one it accepts; but it remains calm and unshockable in the presence of honest confession, trusting the person himself to find his own way to the new life, if only an environment of psychological understanding and gracious forgiveness is provided.

Carl Rogers can describe the attitude of the ideal counselor without using a single religious term, but it is essentially the attitude that good Christian priests and ministers have always intuitively maintained. Anton Boisen expresses the analogy here very clearly: "all psychotherapy thus resolves itself into a matter of confession and forgiveness. It is not so much what the physician says to the patient that matters as what the patient is able to say to the physician. It is dependent not so much upon correct technique as upon an interpersonal relationship of trust on the one side and understanding on the other." [3]

5. *New habits and new associations are needed to make new insights and resolutions into a new life. These grow best in the fellowship of those who have been forgiven and renewed, and who not only keep the convert from relapsing by their support, but offer him a chance to grow strong by serving and strengthening others.* It is quite clear in Alcoholics Anonymous that an unstable new member not only finds better assurance of acceptance here than in any group that has not "been through it," but is upheld by the watchful moral support of his associates, and grows strong by helping new members in his turn. Ideally, any church should offer all-round support to beginners in the Christian life in a similar way, since it is composed of "forgiven sinners" as AA is recruited from reformed or reforming alcoholics. We all know churches which are so deficient in depth of fellowship, or in the attitude of acceptance, or in opportunities for growing by serving, that they do not even remotely correspond

to this description. Such churches are both psychologically and theologically unsound—not proper churches at all.

To summarize, we may say that the part of theology to which the psychological approach can contribute the most is the part dealing with Man, Sin, and Salvation—especially of course on the personal rather than the social side of these doctrines. This was my judgment twenty-five years ago, and it remains unchanged. The exchange of case histories between pastors, and the discussion of the psychological principles involved in good pastoral counseling (such as goes on constantly in the pages of *Pastoral Psychology*) should in the long run help to make these doctrines more precisely and effectually applicable to life than they have sometimes been.

While this is the part of theology most directly affected, the whole of theology is at least indirectly capable of improvement by improved psychological understanding. In my most recent theological work (*Christian Theology: an Ecumenical Approach*, 1955) I arrange all theological doctrines around three angles of a right-angled triangle, symbolizing the fact that they all answer in some way to three basic human needs, that *must* be met somehow: the need of an ultimate Object of trust and devotion (upper acute angle), the need of an ultimate Goal of hope and endeavor (lower right-hand acute angle), and the need of a Way of Salvation whereby man may actually "go to his Goal with the help of his God" (lower left-hand right angle, where the vertical and horizontal lines intersect). Psychology cannot as directly contribute to the doctrines of God and the Kingdom of Heaven as it does to the Way of Salvation: but all these doctrines are finally interrelated. It is a truism, both psychologically and theologically, that a man cannot be "right with God" or "on the way to Heaven" if he is in wrong relationship with himself or with his neighbors. Conversely, a conception of God or of Heaven which is a product of abstract theologism, unrelated to the psychological needs and drives of man, is not a truly religious conception. The God of the Bible is no such abstraction. He is a "very present help in trouble"; and his promises point man to a Chief End to which all of man's psychological drives can be fittingly subordinated. To find God, to "seek first his Kingdom and his righteousness," and to realize true selfhood, are three distinguishable aspects of one indivisible process.

FOOTNOTES

1. Paul Tillich, *Systematic Theology*, I, pp. 40-46.

2. From the mimeographed syllabus of a course on "Christian Faith and Psychology" which Roberts offered at the Ecumenical Institute under the auspices of the Study Department of the World Council of Churches, before *Psychotherapy and a Christian View of Man* was published. The same ideas are more fully developed in the book.

3. *Problems in Religion and Life*, by Anton Boisen (Nashville: Abingdon-Cokesbury, 1946), p. 64.

The Minister and the Psychiatrist: Areas of Mutual Concern

It Is with the Difficulties in Living Common to All People That the Clergyman Has His Most Distinctive Opportunity, and Around Which He Centers His Pastoral Counseling

THE TWO DISCIPLINES most frequently consulted when people are unable to deal helpfully with their deeper feelings are the ministry and psychiatry. Their common areas of concern overlap in their dealings with the troubled person, and it is at this point that both have much to learn from each other. The psychiatrist can contribute his understandings of the deeper motivations and conflicts to which the individual is often exposed, as well as the factors which contributed to the difficulties, and the varied and delicate techniques and basic assumptions by which significant and durable change can be achieved. How-

116

ever, it would equally be expected that the clergyman should be able to share, in this same concern for people, his knowledge and understanding about the relationships which have been life-giving, and the attitudes and means by which people have been able to achieve the abundant life of which Jesus spoke so dramatically: "I came in order that they might have life, and that they might have it more abundantly."

Both disciplines are concerned with the individual's ability to love. The psychiatrist needs to be consulted when the person finds increasing difficulty in being able to love, and indeed has substituted nonloving and even hateful attitudes for loving relationships. The minister's task is to enable the individual to utilize all his powers and needs so that he can realize the most meaningful and satisfying love relationships possible to him. The basic difference might be expressed by saying that the psychiatrist asks the question: "What is preventing this person from being more loving?" The minister asks: "How can this person utilize his ability to be more loving?"

According to Dr. Robert H. Felix, Director of the National Institute of Mental Health of the United States Public Health Service, a recent national survey showed that 40 per cent of all people who sought help for their emotional problems turned first to their ministers. Thus the minister is in a unique position to be of help to troubled persons. Frequently he is on the scene before the problem has developed beyond the incipient stage. Not the least of his opportunities lies in the fact that he is a welcome visitor in the homes of his parishioners, and can thus detect personal problems as they begin to manifest themselves. Hence, opportunities for more adequate understanding of interpersonal processes will prove of inestimable help to the clergyman to do his work more adequately.

One of the first questions which need to be faced and clarified is, Where does pastoral counseling stop and psychiatric therapy begin? No clear-cut, hard-and-fast lines can be drawn at this time, if ever at all, but some guide lines have proved to be very useful. Pastoral counseling has its greatest opportunity in the area that might be called crisis situations. There are certain experiences and feelings associated with birth, growth, maturation, mating, illness, major decisions, retirement, and death, to mention some, which make it highly desirable for the individual to be able to express freely the concerns arising at that time. Where these concerns can be verbalized with a mature, wise individual, whose understandings are solidly anchored in thorough training and satisfying living, a great deal can be done. The minister is in a position not only to stave off the many fears to which the human mind is subject, but, even more, to promote the kind of integration which we know to be needed in wholesome or healthy living. It is with the difficulties in living common to all people that the clergyman has his most distinctive opportunity, and around which he centers his pastoral counseling.

The point at which pastoral counseling ends might be thought of as the point at which the intensity and duration of the problem exceeds the understandings and time available to the clergyman. It has been said, arbitrarily, that when a problem presented to the clergyman has not shown significant change for the better in about ten or twelve interviews, such a problem is usually the kind to require expert referral.

Pastoral counseling has other distinctions. For example, the minister in the role of counselor is grounded in religious faith, which makes a unique kind of relationship and permits him to be much more directive and suggestive. This can prove extremely useful if the counselor's own attitudes are free from authoritarian and manipulative needs. Another distinction is that the pastor can take the initiative in seeking out troubled people rather than having to wait until they come to him. Still another distinction is that when the minister speaks, he does so with the authority of church tradition and the community behind him.

A situation in which these distinctions can be illustrated is in connection with bereavement. Since arrangements for a funeral must be made, the pastor is not only a welcome, but often an expected caller, even by people whose church participation has been sporadic. There are inevitably feelings associated with

the death of someone close: guilt and resentment, pre-
occupations with the image of the deceased, sense of
loss, confrontation with the inevitability of death,
questions about the interpersonal relationship; and
these feelings are so persistent that they demand some
kind of verbalization. Though it is in this situation
that the pastor has one of his most unique opportunities
to be of help, it is precisely here that he must have a
solid understanding of the components of "normal
grief" and the attitudes and techniques by which he
can aid in resolving such situations. Here the excellent
material made available by Erich Lindemann, M.D.,
of Massachusetts General Hospital, can be of inestimable help to the clergyman, especially if presented
by an understanding psychiatrist. Such material would
not only make clear for the clergyman the morbid or
pathological elements in a grief-situation, and hence
enable him to see when a referral is indicated, but it
would encourage him to make available his own services. Religion has always taught the bereaved that
"blessed are they that mourn, for they shall be com-
forted." Hence the mourning processes are encouraged
as a means of dealing realistically with death. It is only
when the bereaved has been able to enter into the
feelings associated with the loss of a love-object that
he can be free to deal with the persistent questions
related to life and immortality.

Since the clergyman is called upon to minister to
people throughout the whole gamut of their life ex-

periences, it would prove helpful to outline the major areas in which problems of pressing concern most frequently become manifest. These areas might be considered fertile ground from which can spring not only the evidences of a mentally healthy, but even more, the mentally mature individual. It is in these areas that the rich clinical experiences of the psychiatrist can offer much understanding and guidance to the minister as he seeks to offer his people the helpful ways of living.

It might well be said that the struggle for mental maturity is either won or lost in the arena of the child's ability to deal with the demands of authority. Here is where we need much clarification as to helpful and nonhelpful child-parent relationships. Of constant concern to the alert pastor are such questions as: What are the basic emotional needs of the growing child? When do parents expect too much and/or too little of their children, and why are such demands made or not made? Out of what attitudes do the constructive and integrative patterns of behavior develop? As an illustration in this area, we can cite the extreme anxiety aroused in some parents by two persistent types of behavior in young children: their almost incessant need to say "no" to just about everything the parent might suggest; and their demanding curiosity and exploration which manifests itself in the many and varied questions youngsters ask, especially in the sphere of sex.

Since the psychiatrist is well aware of the need for just such behavior on the part of the child in order to achieve selfhood, or the dignity of being an individual in his own right, as well as the almost chaotic anxiety evoked in parents by such behavior, a word of explanation to parents can often produce a considerable reduction of their concern that the child is exhibiting antisocial development. Here the sharing of understandings and concerns can and does prove an excellent medium whereby "goodness" in the child's behavior is evoked, not through the imposition of some external and arbitrary standard, but through awareness and acceptance that such "goodness" can be most helpful in the business of living together as humans.

If the individual is to mature, there is much wisdom from the past that needs to be incorporated in one's daily living. However, it is only when the growing individual has come to feel that he has an integrity of his own, that he is respected for what he is—a unique creation—that he can accept the contributions of others. Hence, the attempt to impose the thought and experience of others upon a new generation of individuals often comes to nothing simply because so little attention is given to the unique character of the growing person's own contribution. If education can be a sharing of the wisdom of the past, because it has been meaningful to others in their daily living, and at the same time evoke from the child his own tremendous resources of creativity and originality, then we can draw forth from the child his latent abilities to absorb and to utilize the rich gifts of the past.

It is recognized that there can be no maturity of character unless the growing person has been able to come to terms with the many and varied demands made upon him: social, sexual, vocational, religious, or otherwise. There is much that is good in the world, and much that competes for the individual's attention. It might even be said that the greatest conflict which the individual faces is not the choice between the good and the bad, but between the good and the better. What, then, can produce the kind of integrity that will enable the individual to achieve the responsibility of making up his own mind as to what is helpful and nonhelpful in his living? Here again the sharing of common experiences between religion and psychiatry can contribute a very great deal.

It has been learned by those who have worked intensively with others that, very frequently, a great deal of harm has been done by the inculcating of a sense of shame or guilt about the very basic emotional necessities of human living. Impulses toward tenderness and the expression of feelings of resentment have often been held to be taboo in the name of religion. Obviously, this has resulted in a marked lowering of the individual's self-esteem, since these are feelings which are an inescapable part of being human. To ridicule those who teach such standards, or simply to label them "bad religion," is of little help and only increases the defensiveness of their exponents. What is needed is the opportunity for free discussion of why it is so important that we live up to the expectations of those who are significant to us. This can often do much to help the individual see the destructiveness of such behavior; and the support received through such discussion can often motivate the individual to achieve significant change. Here again, the rich contributions of the clinician, who has worked for a long time, through painful experience, with people who had an intense struggle to effect decisions of their own, can be most salutary to the earnest minister.

Such decisions as choice of vocation and marital partner, and the danger of externally imposed decisions, would provide most fertile ground for discussion between psychiatrist and clergyman.

Hard as it is to make decisions, it is even harder to be willing to re-examine the decisions we have once made, even though additional light and understanding may require a change. But such demands are made upon the maturing and responsible person if he would continue to grow toward selfhood. Much light needs to be shed by those who have witnessed the struggle of many who seemed to prefer the artificial restrictions of a narrow set of religious values. Often these individuals, in their stated adherence to these patterns as "the good," are in just this way avoiding feelings in relationships which have come to be associated with badness. It may well be that these feelings are not bad in themselves, but bad only in a very restricted set of relationships which the individual feels binding upon him. Here the criteria of duration and intensity of the conflicts could offer a helpful means whereby the understanding pastor could make a referral to his psychiatric colleague. Set patterns of behavior, even if given religious sanction, which isolate the individual from his fellows, need serious investigation and change if the person is to achieve spiritual maturity.

It is obvious that, though self-scrutiny must continue, and certain attitudes and behavior patterns will often change, there are some decisions which should remain reasonably secure, such as marital choices and vocational goals. However, it is precisely in these areas that we often find a great deal of vacillating. When one has come to be sure of the ground of one's being, and to have developed some understanding of one's own interpersonal operations, it is to be expected that there will be a considerable continuity in such major life goals as have already been mentioned. The discipline of psychiatry, through its knowledge of the emotional factors which have made for such insecurity of behavior, can aid the struggling pastor to help his people realize the goal of abundant living.

It is felt that those who have done work in the field of group therapy can offer invaluable aid to the pastor in helping him understand and use the resources at his command in the corporate life of the church group, often called the church fellowship. It is in such group relationships that there can often come to be a very healthy sharing of one's deeper feelings and concerns. It has been demonstrated that in group activity one can come to be able to accept oneself and others in a way which is genuinely creative. For some reason things which we could not tolerate in ourselves come to be accepted, thought about, and changed, simply because they have come to us in, and been dealt with through, the group experience.

It is in the group that we can often find the strength to say and do things which would not have been possible to us as individuals. This comes about largely because of one main factor: when such a group is formed, it is clearly recognized that each member is accepted for himself, and as he is, and that he has problems in living. Indeed, the latter reason is just why he is in the group. In such groups the individual finds a maximum of support. Leader and members alike encourage one another, especially in trying situations. Hence, there is attained the much needed security to consider the very things which tend to make life difficult for us as individuals. This again would be an area in which the psychiatrist, through his experience with group dynamics, could make a very helpful contribution to the pastor, and at the same time provide most fruitful opportunities for future collaborative investigation.

As the two disciplines—religion and psychiatry—come together in the mutual sharing of experience and concern in their work with troubled people, it will be discovered that they have much to gain from each other. It is a welcome sign of the times that such sharing is indeed growing among us. As it continues there is every hope that troubled people will find increasing sources of help for their difficulties in living.

must provide effectual opportunities for issue
self-communication.

. . . example, nurses . . . . . . and employers . . .
come to them . . . substantial changes in experience
and concern in their work, which . . . cannot prove to
. . . be discovered that they have failed . . . to gain from
each other . . . a welcome . . . if it is there, then it
. . . being is indeed providing an . . . . It conceives
answers even where the troubled people had had in
seeking sources of help for these difficulties with which
. . . . . .

Prayer

The Efficacy of Prayer

The Religious Person Does Not Seek to
Manipulate the World Through Coercive
Formulas, but Develops Humility Before
an Order Which Is Dynamically Creative

"WHEN WE SET OURSELVES to the work of collecting or re-collecting the scattered pieces of ourselves, we begin a task which, if carried to its natural conclusions, ultimately becomes prayer." [1] Anyone who has studied the great mystics knows how significantly in most of them the process of recollection in the sense just used is related to prayer. An important aspect of its efficacy is at once suggested as is its relation to the normal processes of integration within experience. Efficacy relates in a preliminary way to the genuineness of religion. William James insisted in *The Varieties of Religious Experience* that religion stands or falls by the genuineness of prayer. If nothing happens through prayer, then religion is a delusion.

James referred to more than "subjective influence."
The subjective influence of prayer is not enough, he
affirmed, if prayer and hence religion is to be genuine.
Prayer must liberate energy which operates in both
subjective and objective relationships. James believed
that prayer does release energy which becomes active
in the phenomenal world.

William James' point of view, along with that of
Dr. Sadler, introduces us to most of the problems of
efficacy. The psychological and the philosophical
problem of efficacy are interwoven. From the standpoint of the praying person the efficacy of prayer
involves its genuineness and its validity. James sensed
this when he insisted that the ideal power with which
we feel ourselves in contact in prayer is "something
larger than ourselves." To feeling he assigned a per-
ceptual validity which became part of his doctrine
of radical empiricism. He recognized that any beneficial consequences which flow from praying do not
fulfill the intention or claim of praying unless these
are related to the belief-claims of the prayer.

There are thus vital questions of a most basic sort
which are involved in efficacy. It will not suffice to
catalogue the benefits of prayer, for prayer itself makes
a claim on reality which is the most fundamental aspect of the problem. To say this, is only to recognize
the complexity of the situation. There are obviously
all kinds of prayers. No one would try to defend them
all. Even if all were efficacious in some regard, they

would not be efficacious in the same way. There are obvious differences among physiological, psychological, social, and metaphysical or theological levels of the prayer response and among the kinds of effects which prayers produce. Moreover, we must contrast the special datable acts called praying from the whole life of devotion which may include them. In a preliminary way we may expect a significant difference in efficacy between the outbursts of men and women in a crisis, especially if they do not habitually pray, from that of a saintly devotee.

There is ample evidence from innumerable testimonies that praying has been helpful. The beneficial results reported have referred to all levels of man's relationship to nature, his body, his mind, his fellow men, and God. The physical and biological aspects of human nature have as truly been involved as the moral and the spiritual. In these relationships the efficacy of prayer seems to depend not so much on the words that are used as on the attitude of the self in relation to the object of the attitude. Moreover, in the life of prayer there is generally a development from prayers of desperate outcry or petitions dealing with immediate wants and personal needs, to prayers of thanksgiving, praise and, finally, of communion and union with God. In any event prayer is essentially God directed, that is, it is reality centered. The self acknowledges its dependency on a more-than-human power which has control over its destiny. Though the self may be bowed down in trouble and terribly conscious of its own problems, all prayer finds the encounter with reality such that the latter is central and has the last word. The postulate of the primacy of objective reality is of the essence of the efficacy of praying.

We are led to the recognition, then, that efficacy involves an interpretation, however vague, of the metaphysical context of praying. Assumptions regarding the nature of personal and ultimate reality are bound to enter into any interpretation. These interpretations are often contradictory. If one assumes or otherwise believes that reality beyond man is nonpurposive and impersonal, one is necessarily obliged to limit one's view of efficacy to that of simple reflective meditation or to the role of the God-image which man projects into nature but which is divorced from the validity of the metaphysical idea of God.

Persons who have been taught to pray, though not believing in a personal God or a more-than-human power that is creating and conserving values, may probably experience many of the same benefits as a Christian theist, but the full effects will be different at the level of communion or union. If one assumes that reality is a society of persons, that the Supreme Person is the ground of all finite persons, that he is immanent in his creation and also transcendent over it, the efficacy of prayer will include certain aspects of the prayer life not included in the frame of reference in-

dicated above. The meaning and integrity of intercessory prayer, for example, differs profoundly in an
interpretation which limits community to finite interpersonal relations from one which views all reality as
a society of personal selves. The efficacy of intercessory prayer is not conclusively demonstrated, but it
surely would not be sincerely attempted if the communitarian idea of ultimate reality is rejected.

Prayer postulates the objectivity of reality and at
least an initial and provisional dualism between the
worshiper and God. Reality has the last word. This is
a conception productive of healthy-mindedness. The
religious person develops an attitude in which he does
not seek to manipulate the world through coercive
formulas but one through which he develops humility
before an order which is dynamically creative. In this
respect the person who prays resembles the scientist
and benefits accordingly. The scientist learns the discipline of accepting the priority of objective fact over
subjective idea. It is the idea or hypothesis which is
tested by the objective order. "Nature to be controlled must be obeyed." Nature has the last word
both epistemologically and causally. Since the scientist cannot jump out of his skin he can only compare
a present experience (his hypothesis) by other experiences, so that he never possesses an immediate final
verdict on his ideas. Epistemological dualism seems to
be the actual situation. The gap between idea and ob-

ject is never completely closed. The best idea or hypothesis simply has a higher degree of probability as tested within the context of the community of research than ideas judged to be inadequate or erroneous.

Though the dualism of idea and object persists, the efficacy of scientific processes depends on the faith and willingness of the scientist to submit his thoughts and actions to the verdict of nature whatever that proves itself to be. In the process it is necessary to develop some provisional idea of what nature is within which the exploration and testing takes place. There is ultimately a logical circle which unites postulates and assumptions to hypotheses and inferences. Yet, this circle is transcended by the experimental process and the cumulative body of mutually supporting propositions which have previously been tested. The certitude of the efficacy of a scientific venture is dependent not only on the limited verification of any particular experiment but also on the coherence of mutually supporting postulates and hypotheses in the whole field under investigation.

At the risk of repetition it must be noted that the spiritual disciplines of scientific work have analogies at important points with those of prayer. The cultivation of humility and teachability before reality is one of the chief virtues of mature prayer. To submit to reality raises the self above self-will to objectivity. The almost universal report of prayer is that this reality is not an "it" but a "thou." Many of the ills of mankind are overcome at once when this attitude is taken. Prayer helps men to be willing to face the facts in all areas in which they learn to pray. Reality has a dependably structured process which men learn to accept. This proves to be the case not only with respect to so-called "facts" but with respect to values and norms. Those prayers are most efficacious which have not only the right attitude but which are enlightened by the growing body of scientific and philosophical truth.

Just as the particular techniques and experiments in science depend on the conceptual presuppositions of the field under investigation, so the conceptual presuppositions of the religious man influence his prayer methods. The attitude toward God is crucial. J. B. Pratt's criticism of James Leuba illustrates the point in question. Leuba held that God is valued only as a "meat purveyor." Pratt maintained, on the other hand, that his studies showed that God is valued as an end in himself rather than as a mere means to an end. It is not as a giver, but as a companion that God is valued and sought; it is not his gifts, but himself which the religious soul desires. In so far as God is regarded pragmatically as a giver, it is spiritual benefits that are sought: for example, strength, insight, comfort, courage, and serenity. The valuable subjective effects of prayer depend on the conviction of the objective relation. "If the subjective value of prayer be all the value it has, we wise psychologists of religion had best keep the fact to ourselves; otherwise the game will soon be up, and we shall have no religion left to psychologize about." [2]

The conceptual presuppositions of prayer thus do have a direct bearing on the question of efficacy. Significantly is this true on the higher levels of prayer. When the value of prayer is in the field of a "sense of belonging" or of "communion" or of "companionship," the efficacy of the prayer is directly related to the question of the reality-feeling of divine presence and divine response. Yet, here we must recognize that while many testify to the sense of reality and divine response, others do not do so. Even the greatest mystics learn to carry on in the midst of aridity and the apparent absence of all special benefits.

Many of the benefits of prayer probably have their source in its being a whole response to reality. The more complete the personality response the more values are achieved in and through the experience. There are many correlations between wholeness of response and mental health. Not every prayer is a whole response of the whole person, but prayer grows naturally in that direction in the maturing person; from fragmentary and emergency petitions to acts of devotion that are serene and poised; from partial perspectives to sustained and reflective judgments; from anxious doubts to confident faith in the ground of all hope; from dependence on immediate successes to willingness that the problems be resolved in the larger view; from exclusiveness to inclusiveness; from petty striving to significant life planning; from isolated individual goal-seeking to co-operative communitarian problem solving; from man-centeredness to God-centeredness.

In the wholistic discipline of maturing prayer there is a growth in faith and the capacity for faith; there is a strengthening of inclusive perspectives; there is a deepening of the reality-centered motives; there is a willingness to trust other people; there is a sense of the meaningfulness of existence; there is an expansion of consciousness; there is a growing ability to put oneself in others' places; there is a sense of universal belonging; there is a release of new energies, a purgation of incentives, an overcoming of guilt-feelings, and a release of compassion. Guilt is the sense of alienation. In a well-developed life of prayer the whole activity of the person becomes an act of devotion around a center which is God. As God becomes more real to the praying person the sense of communion becomes more common and with it the assurance that estrangement has been overcome and that all the resources of God are available to the praying person.

In his *Psychology of Religion* Professor Paul E. Johnson lists ten psychological effects of prayer: (1) awareness of needs and realities, (2) confession and harmonious adjustment, (3) trust and relaxation, (4) perspective and clarification, (5) decision and dedication, (6) renewal of emotional energy, (7) social responsiveness, (8) joy, gratitude, and relaxation, (9) loyalty and perseverance, (10) integration of personality. These aspects of efficacy are what one would expect in a situation in which a person in community with others was satisfactorily being related to the Supreme Person. An open consciousness, a learning, dependent, seeking attitude, a willingness to let the ultimate personal reality have the last word, a centering and recollecting of the whole mind around the creative source of all being tends to have this result. These ten effects are clearly related to the whole response of a growing personality to a reality which is taken to be adequate to all one's needs, a reality which leaves one's own person, despite its dependence, respected and loved. With confidence and clarity of mind decisions are made in the light of the values one finds to have relevance and significance for one's problems and those of the community of which one is a part.

A key factor in the efficacy of the prayer experience is the discovery of love and forgiveness. Because God is including in his attitude, man, confronting other men under God, is able to be including in his attitudes. In Christian prayer there is thus more than aspiration; there is a sense of being loved. God takes the initiative. Here belief, the conceptual context of the experience, is important; for the belief in the God of prayer becomes a positive act of faith. God is more than men can believe conceptually; he is the ground they believe in. God responds to men, but the efficacy of their prayers is transcended by him who is more than they can conceive. God is more efficacious than the conceptual beliefs of their prayers provide for as the sun is more efficacious than any theory of sunlight provides for; but without some conceptual framework of relationship the efficacy would be greatly limited.

The problem which now emerges is not whether prayer is efficacious, but what kind of prayer life is truly effectual and in what respects. We have noted that the life of science and the life of prayer are not antithetical if the spiritual process out of which each proceeds in the self is carried to its logical conclusion and becomes humbly involved in the processes of objective reality. Prayer requires discipline and training. The methods we use determine the results we get. Means and ends constitute a whole. The preparation of the consciousness for concentration on the real world, a community of the Divine consciousness and one's fellow men, so that maximum interaction takes place, is essential. There is need for the self to be in an active state of mind. The ground of reality is active process and the self must be properly attuned as active consciousness if it is to grow. It is in relatively passive states of mind that the self fails most frequently. When dull and passive, one is likely to be the victim of all kinds of forces. Passivity is sometimes praised by the mystics, but this is really a paradoxical term referring rather to disciplined receptivity.

The active consciousness in prayer affirms value. Hence it is a state of mind which appreciates values and meanings. It becomes involved in the value-producing activities around it. It seeks to appreciate values in persons, things, and processes, as Wieman says. Anyone who studies the strategy of appreciation knows that it is one of the most effective ways to change from negatively critical to positively constructive activities. People respond to others who are appreciative. The prayers of praise covering the whole realm of God's graces and blessings release the appreciative powers and place the person in a positive relation to other people and to the sources of value.

Efficacious prayer has had a close relation with gratitude. Gratitude involves a due sense of dependence. This acknowledges that the praying individual is not at the center of reality but a recipient of values from others and the Other. The ancients said that gratitude is the mother of the virtues. Thus this aspect of prayer is spiritually efficacious since it overcomes greed and acquisitiveness in the self by the acknowledgment that one is a member of a community in which he receives far more than he ever contributes. Virtues, which are steady habits of the will with respect to various goods, are nourished in a sense of dependence on divine grace.

As this active consciousness develops in appreciation and gratitude it becomes aware of its communitarian lacks. Its needs become more apparent. There develops a humility before facts and problems. Its failures in community living become more obvious. This leads the praying self into a desire to belong to one's fellows and to God on a deeper level than that previously experienced. Private and public worship persisted in provide not only wider perspective but generate a community of concern and an eagerness to overcome one's own faults in order that service can be the more effectively tendered to those in need.

Man is part of a spiritual field tremendously vibrant with new possibilities. He is, as it were, a dynamic participant in an open-ended universe in which values are being created and conserved and in which man can find a meaningful vocation for all his energies. When prayer is directed to God, as in the Lord's Prayer, the meaningfulness of the whole creation is presupposed. In that meaningful whole there is an unending invitation to explore and find and create.

Footnotes

1. William S. Sadler, *The Practice of Psychiatry* (St. Louis, Mo.: G. V. Mosby Company, 1953).

2. James Bissett Pratt, *Religious Consciousness* (New York: Macmillan, 1954), p. 336.

The Influence of Prayer on God and Man

Prayer Involves a Faith and Belief That God Can Be Confidently Expected to Respond to Human Prayer

Among believers in the usefulness of prayer there are two extreme views which must be avoided if its highest developments are to be explained in theory and its chief values sustained in practice.

The first of these views is held by no serious students of the subject but by many superficial and occasional practitioners. This is the belief that prayer is simply and solely the persuading of God to do things which we want done, such as sending rain, curing sick friends, or miraculously replacing our sins with virtues.

The second is the doctrine that prayer never changes anything outside the person who is praying, excepting as the experience of prayer induces him to do things he would not otherwise have done or subjectively realigns the forces in his own personality so as to enable him to do what he otherwise could not have done.

Careful study of the relevant facts can hardly leave a fair-minded person in doubt that to many people prayer brings such subjective effects as clearer insight, relaxation from nervous tension, heightened self-confidence, and increased concern with the well-being of other persons. These psychological results are widely apparent and highly prized, while belief that prayer induces changes in the action of God is beset by theoretical difficulties and is impossible of objective and direct verification. Hence the modern student of religion, particularly the psychologically trained, is tempted to concentrate attention upon the subjective effects, while regarding all thought of influencing God by prayer as ignorant superstition or at best unverifiable and impractical speculation.

However, the notion that it is reasonable to believe in prayer solely for its subjective effects and the changes in human relations and actions which those effects in turn produce is illusory. The reasonableness of prayer for the sake of its subjective effects finally depends on the efficacy of that very kind of prayer most often despised by the sophisticated, namely the petition for divine action.

Prayer implies communication. In poetry, it is true, we may address a tree or star, an ideal, or a mythical monster. Such imaginative procedure often provides a

convenient means of expressing a mood or idea in artistic form. But the impersonal objects addressed are
not expected to hear. The poet does not intend that
they should. The poetry is not written to communicate with them, but with other human beings and to
preserve a vision or mood for the poet himself. Poems
are not really addressed to trees but to people.

Whether we read the prayers of godly men or no-
tice what happens in ourselves in those great, decisive
moments when sudden grief, imminent peril of death,
or overwhelming spiritual joy strips us of all pretense
and sends us to our knees in the most earnest entreaty
or praise to God, we find that true prayer is intended
actually to communicate with him. The projection of
ideals and the imaginative apotheosis of impersonal objects may pass for prayer in some situations, but when
we confront the ultimates of life and really *pray*, we
know at once that true prayer cannot be less than real
communication with another who is "high and lifted
up," supreme in power and the ultimate ground of all
hope.

But if prayer is communication with God it implies
the exerting of an effect on God. If God is not aware
that I am addressing him, then my attempt at communication has failed. If he is aware, then God himself
is having an experience which he would not have had
without my having prayed; in short my prayer has
had an effect upon him. This is not to assume that
God's being is limited to the qualities or the categories

of our own personalities. How much more he is than all we experience or conceive is not here at issue. All that is being insisted is that within all the vast mystery of his being if he is never in any way consciously affected by the utterances of our purposes, then there is no human communication with God and so no prayer.

Moreover, some types of prayer imply effects not only upon God's awareness but also upon his attitudes or actions toward us or our fellows. It will hardly be questioned that when men pray for rain on their parched fields or healing for their distant, dying children, they are expressing at least the hope that their petitions may influence the actions of God. That is precisely why many persons, who think prayer should be valued only for its subjective effects and the fruits of those effects, would doubt that we ought to pray for rain or for the healing of persons beyond the reach of our own ministrations.

It is easy to overlook the fact that prayer of repentance also implies the possibility of influencing God. It is one thing to feel sorry that an act has been committed; it is quite another thing to ask God's forgiveness of that act. Moreover, even though a sinner, in his sorrow over his sin, regrets his sin as a wrong committed *against God*, he is still not praying a prayer of repentance until he asks God to forgive him. But even though he may have complete confidence that God does invariably forgive truly repentant sinners—or rather all the more if he has such confidence—his prayer of repentance implies the potency of prayer to influence God. For certainly to say that God has the same attitude toward the sinner after he has repented as he had before would be to say that he has not forgiven him. If as a consequence of a man's repentant prayer the attitude of God has changed, then man's prayer has influenced a change in God.

Moreover, it has been often observed that the highly desirable subjective changes which frequently follow prayers for divine forgiveness do not follow the mere expression of sorrow for sin. It is precisely the belief that God actually forgives sin which is repented of, that is, belief in the *objective* efficacy of prayer for forgiveness which must be present if its *subjective* efficacy is to be experienced.

Even prayer of communion usually implies belief in an objective effect upon God. To be sure it includes a "practice of the presence of God," a "drawing near" to God on the part of the human aspirant. But it includes also the hope that God will "come" or make his presence and love known. Witnesses to the reality of communion with God testify almost universally to their dependence upon God's action for such high experiences, while at the same time they insist on the necessary condition of man's seeking. Such testimony implies that God's action of making himself known and entering into communion with the human being was influenced by the human prayer, though not controlled by it.

It is hard to see how the subjective values of prayer which are so often lauded, especially among those who have a sympathetic psychological interest in prayer, can be forthcoming without belief in its objective efficacy for the actual changing of God's action. Freedom from a burdensome sense of guilt may be obtained by prayer when it is believed that God actually responds to prayers of repentance by giving forgiveness. Relief from awful loneliness may be experienced in prayer when it is believed that God makes of the prayer a two-way communication and fellowship. Healing of illness is often brought about by prayer when people pray with faith that God sometimes answers human petitions with actual healing. This is an essential reason for the continual refrain among the world's great teachers of prayer that men must pray *with faith*. The faith that is enjoined is not a confidence in a subjective reaction of the prayer upon the person praying. It is faith in *God*, belief that *God* can be confidently expected to respond generously to human prayer.

Observation indicates that when prayer reaches a subjective effectiveness beyond that of mere soliloquy or autosuggestion, it is always accompanied by or rather includes at its very heart the belief that God is aware of the prayer that is being offered and will, or at least may, respond to it. In short, *prayer produces its own distinctive and generally prized subjective results only when it is believed to be capable of bringing about also objective changes in the attitudes or actions of God.*

If this conclusion is accepted, it poses a serious dilemma. To be reasonable we must either believe in prayer for both its effect upon the man praying and its effect on God's attitudes and actions, or we must reject it on both counts. Faced with such a dilemma the first inclination of many an honest student of religion may be to reject prayer altogether on the supposition that there are decisive objections to the belief that prayer ever changes the will of God. To make such a decision would be premature and irresponsible without first carefully appraising the objections on which it would be based. If this appraisal is made it will be discovered that the objections are far less formidable than they appear at first sight. Indeed, they are, I believe, altogether inconclusive. This I hope to show.

1. *The Objection that Natural Law Prevents Response.* In a scientific age when all observable events, possibly excepting acts of human free will, are believed subject to inclusion in a great system of invariable natural law, is it not unreasonable to think that rain might fall or a distant friend be healed because of my prayer? Are the laws of meteorology suspended when prayers are made for rain? Are laws of physiology and

bacteriology sometimes made ineffective when we pray for the sick?

This objection applies particularly to petitions for changes in the physical world. It would be relevant to other types of prayer only if it were supposed that God in his own being were identical with or subject to the laws of nature. In any event the issues are most clearly seen in prayers for physical change, so attention will be concentrated upon those.

The argument that God cannot be expected ever to produce events in the physical world in response to prayer because natural law prevents his doing so is conclusive if he is regarded as fully subject to and bound by natural law. Yet, although human beings cannot suspend the order of nature, they can produce changes in the physical world which would not have occurred without their purposive action. We can cut down forests, join oceans, bridge canyons, turn deserts into gardens, and, alas! turn cities into deserts. In fact, every fully voluntary movement of our bodies is a change in the physical world effected by our purposes. One must have a conception of a very small God to suppose that he is powerless where any one of us is mighty!

Here the argument of the objectors may take a different turn. It may be said that the problem is not of what God *could* do but of what he would and does do. Natural law may be regarded as simply God's orderly ways and yet it may be insisted that his ways *are* orderly without exception. The invariability of his order may be for his pedagogical purposes, providing his children with a reliably predictable setting in which to learn rational thought and responsible action. Although our Father, is he not the Father whose rain and sun fall on just and unjust alike, and whose hurricanes and epidemics of disease do likewise?

Certainly our experience clearly shows that neither a righteous life in general nor prayer in particular offers an easy road to health and prosperity. Many persons, including Jesus of Nazareth, have suffered violent emotional tension, physical agony, and early death, not in spite of their piety but precisely because of their righteous prayers. This is something that much of the more superficial "psychological preaching" overlooks to the deep distress of many spiritually sensitive and thoughtful hearers. To represent religion as a high road to mental and physical comfort is to betray genuine faith and contradict plain truth which ought to be plain to any minister who knows the story of Jesus and his disciples. The tense agonizing of Christ in Gethsemane or the strenuous utterances of Paul bear little resemblance to the peace of mind which many sermons promise as the fruit or the essence of true religion. The peace of God which Jesus promised his disciples was quite different and was not belied by the strenuous lives and early martyrdoms which lay before them.

If righteousness and prayer do not guarantee health

or comfort to those whose lives they fill, then surely prayer for the health of *other* persons does not guarantee that health will be given. But this is not to say that God never responds by giving health, by sending rain, or by other ministrations to those in whose behalf petitionary prayers are offered. Moreover, we must not exclude the possibility that sometimes he responds to the prayer by acts radically different from those asked but nevertheless *responds*, doing what he would not have done had prayer not been offered.

But would not such responses constitute violations of natural law? And would they not therefore contradict the most assured knowledge of a systematic causal order of events in predictable sequence? Do not the sciences show that God does not, in fact, act in ways unpredictable apart from the knowledge of who is praying and for what favor?

To all these questions the answer must be a firm *No*. Great achievements have been made possible through the formulas of prediction which the sciences have developed. But the formulas themselves are abstractions which never quite precisely fit the facts of the real world excepting as approximations. The discovery that this is true, not merely because of our ignorance, but because of the nature of reality, has constituted one of the most important themes in the development of physics through the last fifty years. It has not destroyed the practical usefulness of science but has actually enhanced it. The statistical probabilities which are attainable are sufficient for innumerable practical purposes, and it has proved useful to know also something about the limits of predictability in some spheres, particularly in the study of subatomic units.

But practically useful as statistical probabilities and approximations are, they do not enable us to say that God cannot respond to our prayers by significant change in the physical order of events. Laplace supposed that the natural order was so rigid that if we could know all the causal laws and the present disposition of every material particle in the universe, including its velocity and direction of movement, we could predict every event which would ever occur. The new physics has shown Laplace to have been in error, not merely because we could not know enough or compute sufficiently well—for he would have acknowledged these human shortcomings readily enough—but because the universe is not that sort of closed and rigid system. The belief that God invariably acts in a way which would not have been predictable by anyone knowing enough about the laws of nature, without taking into account our prayers, is a belief which the sciences cannot prove and from the proof of which modern physics has moved much further away.

It seems reasonable to regard natural law as a system of predictable limits within which God moves. But though these limits are exceedingly narrow in the case of specifically abstracted events, the cumulative effect of many deviations within those limits, particularly in such complex subsystems as a human body or the interplay of events affecting the weather, may often be physically considerable and for practical effect of crucial significance.

If we were to possess a really complete account of events in our physical order, it would certainly have to include the purposive acts of human beings. Is it not reasonable to believe that it would have also to include the purposive acts of God? Within the purposes of God predictable order apparently stands high, but we have no reason to think that it stands alone as his one all-determining consideration.

2. *The Objection That God Knows Best and Does Best Without Our Prayer.* Probably all who believe that God is a personal being who knows when we pray believe also that he is far wiser and better than we. He must know more surely than we what is best for us and for other people. If he is truly *God* he does not need our urging to do the best possible for all his children. What good effect, then, can our prayers possibly have in the influencing of his action? If, strangely, we should be able to persuade him to change his own plans for us, would not the result be his doing something beneath his loftiest purpose, something less than the best?

Kept in this high degree of abstraction, the objection looks decisive. It seems to indicate that any influence our prayers might have on God's action would be a bad influence and hence the good God in his wisdom must protect us from ourselves by refusing to be thus influenced.

But wait! Not so fast! What is this best which God was intent on doing before we prayed? Was it some timeless, changeless object, like the Platonic Ideas, above and independent of all human experience and the changes of our temporal order? How far beyond human experience God's purpose may reach we do not know. But so far as we and our prayers are concerned with his action, is not *the best* which he seeks precisely the best for us and our fellows? Is the best for every nation the same? Surely it is, indeed, best for every man and nation to be included among the obedient faithful company in his divine kingdom. But is the best next step toward the highest goal the same for everyone and at every time? Is not the best that God can do for anyone a changing quantity, changing according to the place where that one stands in his development at the time? Moreover, in view of the inextricably social nature of our existence and the profoundly social character of God's goal for us, is not the best for *any* one at any given time dependent on the place where *everyone* stands at that time? Is it not especially dependent on the relationship which every other person bears to that individual and to God at that time?

When I pray, I change the situation with which God has to deal. As far as certain specific events are concerned, what was the best he could do for me or for my friends before I prayed may still be the best now in this changed situation. But it may not. God must confront many and complex considerations, concerning the need for maintaining a reliable order of law, the need for teaching us all our dependence upon each other and upon him, and many other matters known or unknown to us. With all this in view, in a situation where one or more persons are praying earnestly for my sick friend, perhaps it is better that he should be healed. On the other hand, without the prayer it might have been better for him to continue in illness or even to be taken from this world.

We cannot know, when we pray, what the results will be—whether pleasure or pain, health or illness. But we can know that in the coinage of eternal values, the best that God can do for us and others is better when we pray than when we do not. If we pray that the cup of agony and death be removed and it is instead given to us, brimming over, there will still be greater redemptive power in the agony after prayer than in long life without prayer.

Even a human father, confronted by changed attitudes and relationships among his children, knows that what is best for them has now changed. How much more must our Father in heaven know this!

3. *The Objective That God Is the Sovereign Other Unaffected by Our Little Acts.* Closely related to the thought that we have been discussing, yet of distinct

character, is a yet more abstract objection, based not on God's superior wisdom or goodness but on his divine sovereignty.

If we think of God as truly the creator or ground of all being, we must know that "His ways are not our ways." Much of his purpose is veiled in mystery. His power and knowledge so far transcend our own as to make our little lives seem infinitesimal and helpless by comparison. Are we to suppose that he who holds the galaxies in their places is to be moved in his course by our puny deeds or words?

In response it must be observed that size and magnitude of power are poor clues to worth. A single child seeking to fathom the mysteries of starlight is worth more than millions of light years of unfeeling space or the vast electronic furnaces of distant suns. Now it is precisely the daring affirmation of Christian faith that God does care for every person and that a little child is precious in his thought.

Even so, though he loves each one of us, does he not remain the sovereign God while we are but the grateful or ungrateful recipients of his mercy? Do we not forget our place when we think that we can influence his action?

There is only one condition which could make it reasonable to think that anything in human life could significantly influence the acts of God. But it is reasonable to believe in such influence if God himself wills that we should be the bearers of such responsibility. To deny that he could give to us this power is to belittle him, not to show a superior regard for his majestic sovereignty. To deny that he does do so is to deny that he loves us enough to seek for us the maturing of real, responsible stewardship.

The argument here given has been necessarily fragmentary. Indeed, all of our evidence is fragmentary. But if our argument has led in the right direction a number of conclusions would seem to be in order. They are offered to the reader as propositions for his own thought, testing by experience and amendment in the light of more prayer and further evaluation.

1. God includes prayer and the fellowship of faith and mutual concern within his purpose for all mankind. This purpose uses the causal order as a means and hence includes but transcends it.

2. When we pray we present to God a situation significantly changed, in relation to his purpose for us, from the situation which he confronted before we prayed.

3. In that changed situation the best that He can do for us is significantly altered. Even in relation to a specific act, as of healing or sending rain, his action may therefore be influenced.

4. Petitionary prayer may not bring health, wealth, or pleasure, but pain, privation, and lonely sorrow—as it did for Jesus. But because prayer is according to God's purpose it heightens the best possibilities for us.

God may not give what we ask, but he will give better gifts to us and our fellows when we ask than when we do not.

5. Every true prayer implies, if it does not make explicit, the spirit of Jesus' words, "not my will but Thine be done." For it would be superstitious effort to practice magic if we sought to impose our wills upon God.

6. The higher subjective values of prayer, its most worthily praised effects upon the life of the person praying, are gained only when we pray with faith in its objective efficacy, that is, its influence upon God's own action.

7. On the other hand, the influence of prayer upon God's action cannot be reasonably defended unless the prayer is at the same time changing the person praying. A careless saying of prayer words which involved no soul-searching act of faith would not offer to God a significantly changed human situation and could not be intelligently thought to affect his acts toward men.

These two efficacies of prayer, that is, its changing of the person praying and its influencing the will of God, are clearly illustrated from the very beginning of the Lord's Prayer, along with their profound and inextricable relationship to each other. In the midst of all the fear and strife of earth, we cannot say, "Our Father" and mean it, without being deeply changed from the prevailing spirit of human society. But a

the same time, to address "Our Father" is to affirm
that altogether before and beyond ourselves there is
another who cares what we say to him from our hearts.
He can be counted on to give the bread of life and
not a stone to all who ask of him in faith.

A Psychological Understanding of Prayer

Prayer Is a Dynamic Experience of Harmony Within and Without That Heals Conflict and Loneliness

PRAYER is the most needed and neglected practice in modern life. Why is prayer needed? Because human life in our time is one crisis after another, for which we are not adequately prepared. Never in the memory of man has human life been so insecure, and never have people tried so frantically to defend themselves against dangers. Military preparedness has now come to be the chief business of national governments, and foreign policies are shaped primarily toward collective security to allay the fear of possible enemies. We insure our property against every conceivable risk such as fire, storm, collision. Most of us carry life insurance, accident and disability insurance, health and hospital insurance, as well as insurance to cover unemployment and old age through state and federal provisions for social security. Yet in spite of all this we are anxious and insecure, tense and apprehensive at every thought of failure, disaster, and loss.

With all this preparedness you would logically expect us to be the most secure people in the history of the world. But instead we are calling for more and more defenses to save us from more and more dangers. When the visible dangers are prepared for we worry about the invisible dangers; when the known risks are provided against we are disturbed by threats of the unknown. Consequently we live under a diffuse cloud of generalized anxiety and unrelieved distress which distorts our perspective, disturbs our health, undermines public confidence, and robs our peace of mind. The more we prepare the less security we enjoy, which evidently means that our preparations are in vain. Why is this so? Evidently, because we prepare against external dangers by external defenses, while neglecting inner preparations to cope with the inner turmoil that continues unabated in the midst of all the façades of military might and protective precautions.

Is there no escape from these haunting anxieties that pursue us like avenging furies? Is there no relief from this high-pressure living that is driving us to distraction? Where can we find surcease from the burden of overcrowded stimuli we invite to hide our emptiness, even a few moments to rest from the din of

loudspeakers, bells, and whistles or the flashing lights
and scenes of billboards, neon signs, and television?
How can we meet other persons on the level of
equality and fraternity, without the off-balance of
inferiority and superiority, as we mingle in a competitive society and struggle for recognition and
status? Caught as we are in conflicts of desire and
aversion, trapped by dilemmas of painful indecision
and cross-purposes, is there no better way out of our
confusion and despair?

Yes, there is *prayer*. But who has time to pray when
there are so many urgent things to do, so many important gains to make before it is too late, if time has
not already run out and left us unprepared for the
next emergency? This frantic mood of hurry and
worry is not the mood of prayer. Who in our speed-
ing age is not caught in the headlong rush of crowds
thronging and pushing to and fro? Who is not in-
fected by the contagion of violent haste in the modern tempo of making a living, getting ahead, making
progress, and arriving ahead of schedule, which is the
insatiable excitement of our time? With all our labor-
saving and time-saving devices we are busier than ever,
for somehow we feel driven compulsively to go and
get there. If a man's vocation is a pursuit, so is his va-
cation, his traffic and shopping, his social events and
recreation, his reading and leisure-time. Have you at-
tended prayers lately, with one eye on the clock and

the other on the commuters' train schedule; or did you have to give up the once hallowed tradition in the mad rush of getting the family up and through the bathroom to a bite of breakfast in the kitchen, before dashing out the door to keep ahead of the "Don't-be-late" schedule?

Living at this nervous pace is undoubtedly one of the dangers we are trying to escape, if we value our health or serenity. And prayer, contrary as it is to the anxious haste of our daily regimen, might as well be the antidote to its insidious poison, exactly what we need to clarify our confusions and heal the anguish of soul that saps our vitality and dims our perspective. If this is a reasonable hypothesis that prayer is what we need most, then why is prayer so neglected as it is today?

Prayer is neglected because it is misunderstood. It is mistaken by some for a magical, mechanical trick whereby repeating a formula or going through mechanical motions of a prayer wheel or rosary, one can cheat the laws of cause and effect and beat the game by avoiding the requirements of an orderly universe. Others misrepresent prayer as begging favors from an unwilling God as Abraham bargained for Sodom, or Jacob received his blessing by favoritism and, noting how prayers often seem to be unanswered, decide they will not wait upon the caprices of a fickle though divine autocrat. Others misconstrue prayer as reminding God of his neglected duties, telling him what he ought to know without such reminders and well-worn petitions on behalf of various and sundry affairs on earth. To those who view prayer in these ways, it is often rejected as unscientific, unethical, and unnecessary. Consequently, to a considerable number of our contemporaries prayer is disbelieved and discounted as of little value.

If prayer is to serve most effectively in meeting the distresses of modern life, a fresh approach will be needed. How shall we understand prayer psychologically? Prayer is a dynamic experience of harmony within and without that heals conflict and loneliness in renewing one's sense of belonging to a larger wholeness. We may not agree as to the exact nature of this larger wholeness to which we seek a relationship of dynamic wholeness. To those who work and think in the framework of natural science, this wholeness may appear as a Process so much vaster than our little minds that we cannot define it in our terms or concepts, yet to which we are drawn as iron filings to a magnet or a compass to the North Pole. To those who are oriented to the New Testament tradition of Christianity this cosmic wholeness will be most meaningful as a Heavenly Father who faithfully loves and cares for his earthly children, and whom to know in this redemptive and forgiving love is life of eternal significance. From either point of view, we seek in prayer to approach as earnestly and reverently as possible the

Universal Thou, who is somehow in ways we are too feeble to comprehend, forever responsive to human need and reaching toward us as we reach toward him in creative and sustaining value-making and value-sharing energies.

As in love life is devoted to life, so in prayer I seek "Thou" trusting that "Thou" is seeking me, and through this conscious effort to establish an I-Thou relationship, we may experience a deepening sense of integration and communion.

When it is so experienced, prayer is reverent self-transcendence, arising from finite loneliness, the need to belong to a larger wholeness, and hunger to realize an I-Thou relationship which is the source of value-creativity. Prayer is one of the ways in which a self reaches out beyond its lonely separation to find harmonious and creative relationships. It is distinguished from other outreaches by a desire to reach the ultimate source of Creativity and establish thereby an I-Thou relationship with the centrality of being from whose productivity values arise.

What will prayer accomplish? As a scientist goes to his laboratory with an open and searching mind, so the one who prays comes to experiment reverently with the ultimate mysteries of responsive reality. Each will search in his own way to comprehend the mysteries of communion with "Thou," and not until then will he attempt to communicate what his experimental

praying reveals to him. Even then he may not be able
to communicate his findings successfully, for we converse most readily at superficial levels, and the deeper
the experience of mystery, the more wordless it will
be in the unique significance of its emotionality. Whatever we may say in our groping efforts to describe the
meaning of such communion will surely be almost infinitely inadequate. But something may be said to
sketch in barest outline the elementary possibilities of
genuine prayer.

What psychological effects may we expect from
prayer? It is the testimony of those who practice it
most faithfully that prayer develops trusting attitudes
of *relaxation* to release nervous tensions, reduce anxieties, and open new resources of hope and confidence.
Another characteristic resultant of prayer is the *insight* that comes of facing reality honestly in a larger
perspective of ultimate values and eternal destinies,
where one may come to "believe the centuries against
the hours," as confusions and prejudices yield to a
calmer view when all things are considered. Prayer is
a way of choosing the mood and shaping one's disposition by the *positive suggestion* of what we most
desire to affirm. Prayer has been called dominant desire, and there can be no doubt that desires bring results. "All that we are is the result of what we have
thought," says the Buddhist proverb; and the Hebrew
equivalent is no less true, "As a man thinketh in his
heart, so is he." Prayer is not complete until it comes

to *decision* and the release of dammed-up energies into open channels of constructive action, thereby resolving the conflicts and frustrations of indecision by dedicating oneself to a larger purpose and *renewing* life at its creative source in this dynamic relationship.

If these psychological changes are effective, prayer will also have social consequences. If communion is a dynamic relationship, it will evidently change my relation to God in seeking to adjust myself to cosmic perspectives and purposes. To Job, who was tempted to curse God and die, prayer brought a turning point where he was able to hope that life could be better and know that patience may win over adversity. To Paul breathing out threatenings and violence, a prayer of "Lord, what wilt thou have me to do?" changed the whole course of his life and the history of Christianity. Such prayer moves the center of one's life from *I* to *Thou* and then to *We*.

Prayer when effective will radically change all of one's relationships. If it changes my relation to God, that will immediately change God's relation to me. The best things I may desire cannot happen to me until I am willing, for unconscious resistance will otherwise block the way as in neurotic conflicts and psychosomatic illness. The creative work of growth and healing will take place only when one is actually ready and open for it and harmoniously related thereto. Family quarrels and hostile attitudes may be self-perpetuating and self-defeating until some new resource for forgiving love comes into play through prayer. For prayer changes my relations to other persons in creative ways. Why pray for enemies and those in need? Essentially because I can no longer be indifferent or hostile to those who are united with me in the genuine good will of honest prayer. Why pray for friends? To draw our hearts together in love and make a brotherhood that is deeper than blood or self-interest.

How shall we pray with psychological understanding for health? Not with fretful anxiety and petulant protest, but with confidence and thankful gratitude for the quiet miracle of healing growth. How pray for wisdom? Not with argumentation for my imperious desires, but with listening attitudes open to change one's mind and see beyond one's prevailing prejudices. How pray for love if tense and insecure or resentful and blaming? Not with jealous demands or fearful anxieties but with empathy to put yourself in his place and feel what he feels, so as to understand and forgive all, to show affection and loving-kindness in attitude and deed. How pray for peace in a world of mounting threats and suspicions? Not by begging God to save us against our enemies or give victory and power to those on our side, but seeking rather to yield pride and possession enough to meet on common ground, to go more than halfway in a generous spirit desiring their welfare as ardently as our own, in all humility acknowledging our mistakes and asking how we can do the things that make for peace and mutual helpfulness.

Such praying will not be easy or natural for us who are steeped in the anxieties and struggles for power which are the thorns and thistles of our pride. Yet if any generation needed the curative and regenerating energies of prayer it is we who are standing in the need of prayer. Out of the depth of our anguish and the urgency of this need we may decide to pray that we may learn how to pray.

Prayer

Prayer Fulfills the Function of Self-Renewal by Making One's Experience Consciously Social [1]

THE SPECIFIC and characteristic process by which the worshiper's valuations are reorganized or confirmed and taken as a divine response is that of suggestion. He who prays begins his prayer with some idea of God, generally one that he has received from instruction or from current traditions. He commonly retires to a quiet place, or to a place having mental associations of a religious cast, in order to "shut out the world." This beginning of concentration is followed by closing the eyes, which excludes a mass of irrelevant impressions. The body bows, kneels, or assumes some other posture that requires little muscular tension and that may favor extensive relaxation. Memory now provides the language of prayer or of hallowed scripture, or makes vivid some earlier experience of one's own. The worshiper represents to him-

172

self his needs, or the interests (some of them happy ones) that seem most important, and he brings them into relation to God by thinking how God regards them.

The presupposition of the whole procedure is that God's way of looking at the matters in question is the true and important one. Around God, then, the interests of the individual are now freshly organized. Certain ones that looked large before the prayer began now look small because of their relation to the organizing idea upon which attention has been focused. On the other hand, interests that express this organizing idea gain emotional quality by this release from competing, inhibiting considerations. To say that the will now becomes organized toward unity and that it acquires fresh power thereby is simply to name another aspect of the one movement. This movement is ideational, emotional, and volitional concentration, all in one, achieved by fixation of attention upon the idea of God. This, as far as structure is concerned, is simply autosuggestion. It is directly in line with autosuggestion of health, and it is just the reverse of the autosuggestion of weakness, which leads toward sin, and of the autosuggestion of sickness, that disarranges various physiological functions.

It is sometimes said that faith is a prerequisite for success, whether in prayer or in autosuggestion of health. Therefore, when success occurs where there is contrary suggestion or lack of confidence, the inference is drawn that here a foreign cause, not autosuggestion, is the explanation. But the supposition that faith is prerequisite is faulty at the best. Many a person, skeptical of the powers of a hypnotizer, has submitted himself as a subject in the expectation of utterly "resisting the influence," but has been astounded to find himself a follower of the operator's suggestions just like credulous subjects. Faith-healing and mental-healing cults often win adherents by producing physical relief in the as yet unconvinced. At revival meetings scoffers are sometimes brought to their knees in spite of their unfaith. Just so, surprising reversals sometimes take place in prayer, faith being there born or reborn, instead of being merely exercised.

What is prerequisite in all these cases is not a particular expectation, but a particular direction of attention. Merely repeating certain sentences with attention to their meaning, but regardless of their truth or falsity, will sometimes result in marked control of further mental processes. Persons who have been troubled with insomnia, or wakefulness, or disturbing dreams, have been enabled to secure sound sleep by merely relaxing the muscles and repeating mechanically, without effort at anything more, some formula descriptive of what is desired. The main point is that attention should fix upon the appropriate organizing idea. When this happens in a revival meeting one may find one's self unexpectedly converted. When it happens in prayer one may be surprised to find one's whole mood changed from discouragement to courage, from liking something to hating it (as in the case of alcoholic drinks, or tobacco), or from loneliness to the feeling of companionship with God.

The internal conversation that constitutes prayer is not an isolated thing, but a specific instance of a general form of mental procedure. Thinking as a whole has the same form. Not merely does rudimentary thinking, which is impulsive and emotional, involve the assumption of reciprocal attitudes between the thinker and his objects, but even the more cautious and controlled sort that weighs considerations, and advances from position to position, moves on in the form of question and answer, proposal and counterproposal, internal debate, and final agreement of the debaters. More than this; considered from the standpoint of mental structure only, my intercourse with my fellows also is internal conversation, a give-and-take, both sides of which are in a way accessible to my own introspection.

This analysis of the structure of prayer has already touched upon some of its functions. It is a way of getting one's self together, of mobilizing and concentrating one's dispersed capacities, of begetting the confidence that tends toward victory over difficulties. It produces in a distracted mood the repose that is power. It freshens a mind deadened by routine. It reveals new truth, because the mind is made more elastic and more capable of sustained attention. Thus does it remove mountains in the individual and, through him, in the world beyond.

Prayer fulfills this function of self-renewal largely by making one's experience consciously social, that is, by producing a realization that even what is private to me is shared by another. Burdens are lightened by the thought that they are burdens to another also, through his sympathy with me. This would be a gain even if I were not sure that this friend would remove the burden from my shoulders. The values of prayer in sickness, distress, and doubt are by no means measurable by the degree to which the primary causes thereof are made to disappear. There is a real conquest of trouble even while trouble remains. Now and then the conquest is so precious that one rejoices in the tribulation itself as a friendly visitation. It is sometimes a great source of strength, also, merely to realize that one is fully understood. The value of having some friend or helper from whom I reserve no secrets has been rendered more impressive than ever by the Freud-Jung methods of relieving mental disorders through (in part) a sort of mental housecleaning, or bringing into the open the patient's hidden distresses and even his most intimate and reticent desires.

Into the psychology of the healings that are brought about by this psychoanalysis we need not go, except to note that one constant factor appears to be the turning of a private possession into a social possession, and particularly the consciousness that another understands. I surmise that we shall not be far from the truth here if we hold that, as normal experience has the *ego-alter* form, so the continuing possession of one's self in one's developing experience requires development of this relation. We may, perhaps, go as far as to believe that the bottling up of any experience as merely private is morbid.

But, however this may be, there are plenty of occasions when the road to poise, freedom, and joy is that of social sharing. Hence the prayer of confession, not only because it helps us to see ourselves as we are, but also because it shares our secrets with another, has great value for organizing the self. In this way we get relief from the misjudgments of others, also, and from the mystery that we are to ourselves, for we lay our case, as it were, before a judge who does not err. Thus prayer has value in that it develops the essentially social form of personal self-realization.

Moreover, where the idea of God has reached high ethical elevation, prayer is a mode of self-assurance of the triumph of the good, with all the reinforcement that comes from such assurance. Confidence in ultimate goodness may support itself upon various thought structures. Many Christians attach their thought of God and of a meaningful world to Jesus as the revealer and worker-out of the divine plan. With him

as leader they feel that they cannot fail. Others attach
their ethical aspirations directly to God, who may then
be thought of as present with the worshiper in these
very aspirations. Others think of the world purpose
in less sharply personal terms, as the evolution of the
cosmos toward a moral life that was not, and now is
only beginning to be, but is nevertheless the inmost
law of the system. In the last case prayer shades off
from conversation toward mere contemplation, yet
without failing to identify the individual's own purpose with a world-purpose that is moving toward sure
fulfilment.

In all these types of self-assurance the individual
may do little more than apply to himself by suggestion
an idea that is current in the cult with which he is
familiar. Yet the idea that is thus applied grows in the
process of appropriating it to one's self. It has, in fact,
been generated in men in and through prayer. That is
to say, prayer is a process in which faith is generated.
It is a mistake to suppose that men assure themselves
of the existence and of the character of God by some
prayerless method, and then merely exercise this ready-
made faith in the act of praying. No, prayer has
greater originality than this. Alongside of much tra-
ditionalism and vain repetition there is also some
launching forth upon voyages of exploration and some
discovery of lands firm enough to support men when
they carry their heaviest burdens.

To complete this functional view of prayer we must

not fail to secure the evolutionary perspective. If we glance at the remote beginnings, and then at the hither end, of the evolution of prayer, we discover that an immense change has taken place. It is a correlate of the transformed character of the gods, and of the parallel disciplining of men's valuations. In the words of Fosdick, prayer may be considered as dominant desire. But it is also a way of securing domination over desire. It is indeed self-assertion; sometimes it is the making of one's supreme claim, as when life reaches its most tragic crisis; yet it is, even in the same act, submission to an overself. Here, then, is our greater problem as to the function of prayer. It starts as the assertion of any desire; it ends as *the organization of one's own desires into a system of desires recognized as superior and then made one's own.*

At the beginning the attitude is little more than that of using the gods for men's ends; at the culmination prayer puts men at the service of God for the correction of human ends, and for the attainment of these corrected ends rather than the initial ones. Like everything else in religion, prayer has several lines of development. Every religion has its own characteristic ways of approaching its divinity or divinities, and its own characteristic valuations are expressed thereby. All, however, as we may be sure from our whole study of religious evolution, reflect the notion of society then and there prevailing. In the Christian religion, with its central emphasis upon love, prayer tends to become, wherever the constructive significance of love has not been submerged by ritualism or dogmatism, the affirmation of what may be called social universalism of essentially democratic tendency. On the one hand, the act of praying now becomes highly individual. To be prayed for by a priest is not enough, nor does mechanical participation in common prayer suffice.

Whether one prays with others or alone, one is required to pray in one's own spirit, and to do it sincerely. Paradoxical as it may seem, this throwing of the individual back upon himself, with insistence that he here and now express his very self, produces, not individualistic desire, but criticism of desires from a social point of view. Here self-assertion becomes self-overcoming in and through acceptance of the loving will of the Father as one's own. Now, because the Father values so highly every child of his, in prayer to him I must adopt his point of view with respect to my fellows, desiring for each of them full and joyous self-realization. This sort of submission—to a God who values each individual—tends therefore toward the deference for each individual that is the foundation of democracy. Here the function of prayer is that of training men in the attitudes of mind that are fundamental to democratic society.

Finally, prayer has the function of extending one's acquaintance with agreeable persons. Here and there, at least, men enjoy God's companionship just because of what he is, without reference to benefits that he may bestow. This pure friendship sometimes includes the joy of helping the Great Friend. It is true that when philosophy identified God with some abstract absolute the notion of helping him is ruled out. But religion is different from philosophy. As a rule the gods of religion—and not less the God of Christianity—stand to their worshipers in a relation of mutual give and take. As a primitive group feeds its god in order to make him strong, and rejoices and feasts with him as an invisible guest, so in Christianity God and men stand in mutual need of each other.

This must be so if God is love. Men are saved by grace alone, but there is joy in heaven over one sinner who repents; men are called into the family of God, yet only as men fulfill fraternal relations with one another can God have the satisfactions that belong to a father. Thus it is that Christian prayer has to be reciprocal as between God and worshiper. There is an ancient doctrine that our prayers are inspired in us by God himself, so that he also prays in our prayers. That is to say, at this point each of the two, God and the worshiper, finds himself by identifying his own desire with that of the other.

This is the culmination of the self-and-*socius* consciousness that makes us persons. The function of prayer at this level, then, is to produce (or, as the case may be, sustain) personal life, which is also social life, as something of ultimate worth.

Footnote

1. This is the second half of the chapter on prayer from Coe's *Psychology of Religion* (Chicago: University of Chicago Press, 1916). Reprinted by permission.

SPIRITUAL HEALING

The Relation of Religion and Health

Healing in the Spiritual or Genuine Religious Sense Is Mediated by Faith [1]

From earliest times to the present, three ways of healing are recognized in the source literature: religious or spiritual healing, magic or psychic healing, and bodily or natural healing. Each of these concepts is not only vague in itself, but there is a continuous confusion and overlapping of them, and, still more striking, a permanent attempt on the part of each to swallow up the others. Examples for the distinction as well as the confusion of the three ways of healing are abundant in both ancient and modern times. The Assyrians and Babylonians distinguished, without separating them however, the religious element in healing, which consisted for them in sacrifice and prayer directed toward beings of a superhuman character, the magic element, consisting in mutual sympathetic influence between human and cosmic forces, and the natural element, consisting in drugs or the knife.

The Persians distinguished the "word-doctor" from the "herb-doctor" and the "knife-doctor." About the first they said: "This one is the best of all healers who deal with the Holy Word, and he will best drive away sickness from the body of the faithful." The "Holy Word," here, is obviously a religious word with magic power, showing the mixture of religion and magic in a form which always remained very important: the *word*. (The Persians gave us the term "magic.") But Origen, also, says: "It is not the thing signified, but the qualities and peculiarities of words which possess a certain power for this or that purpose." Therefore, he asserts, no other word should be used for God than the word God, and no other spiritual healing is possible than through the use of the name, Jesus Christ. What is religious, what is magic in this kind of healing?

Jumping to the present, we find the distinction of the three ways of healing precisely expressed by Hiltner when he says:

> In some cases the surgeons must cut out offending tissue in order to release the forces of healing, in other cases personality analysis is the central need, and in still other cases conscious recognition of the divine power of the healing influences is most needed. In the majority of cases, something of all three may be helpful. We know more about when the surgeon's knife or a drug or a new diet is needed, than we know about the others. We know more about when personality analysis is needed than we do about when prayer is needed.

This sounds not very different from the old Persian text, except that they knew more about the herb and word medicine than about the knife. But again we must ask: what is the relation of the realms presupposed by the three ways of healing? What is religious, and what is psychic?

The mixture of the three in a religious formulary is illustrated in the old Christian Sacramentary of Serapion, where the following prayer accompanies the unction of the sick:

> We pray Thee send out a healing power of the only-begotten from heaven upon this oil, that it may become to those who are being anointed with it, for a throwing off of every disease and infirmity, for a protection against every demon, for a removal of every unclean spirit, for a driving out of all fever and shivering fit, for good grace and remission of sins, for a medicine of life and salvation.

Here, demons, fever, and sins are united, and the healing power from heaven is to be united with the sacred oil. The religious, the psychic, and the natural are completely mixed. Is there a distinction? The same mixture appears in a tractate of Paracelsus concerning the Lord's Supper, where, however, the approach is from the side of the natural element in healing. For Paracelsus, bread and wine are natural powers, yet sacred by nature's divine character of growth, *before* they enter the sacrament. Again, the natural, the magical, and the religious are also united, when he says:

"The true religion of the physician is that he first of all knows and understands all nature in its growth, the inner character of each," and about the inner character, he adds: "Therefore, he is a philosopher, who if he knows something in one thing, knows the same also in another thing." This last is magic knowledge, yet for Paracelsus it is, at the same time, philosophy of nature and religion. Is there any way of clearing up these confusions and overlappings?

It cannot be denied that religious healing, in the strict sense of the word, was united with magical and natural healing everywhere in the ancient world. The great physicians of the legendary past were deified: Imhotep in Egypt, Asklepios in Greece, Thrita in Persia, and so on. Moreover, the centers of healing power were medical temples, such as those of Isis, Asklepios, and, later, certain Christian churches, such as SS. Cosma e Damiani in Rome. The physicians were the priests, or rather the priests were physicians, for the religious aspect did not preclude the use of drugs, medicinal springs, diet, and even surgery. But more important was the magical side, and this in pagan and Christian temple-resorts alike. The practice of incubation, or sleeping in the sacred precinct, during which the healing god appears in a vision for which the patient has been psychologically prepared, shows a typical admixture of magic and religion. The same appears in the use of votive offerings, talismans, incantations, name-magic, and so on in the process of healing. Both empirical medicine and real psychological insight were developed in connection with these practices.

I want to suggest definitions of the religious, the magical, and the natural way of healing, in order to disentangle some of these age-old confusions without doing violence to the complexity of the situation. Indeed, I want to show also why the theoretically clear distinctions are so difficult of application to reality. That the confusions persist in contemporary thinking is very plain. Thus, Dawson writes: "Healing in all its branches has always been . . . a process requiring the combination of scientific and religious factors." To prove this he cites, for example, the "faith-healing" of witch doctors. But this is just the question, whether such magical healing can be called real "faith-healing," instead of healing by suggestion, and whether it should not be sharply distinguished from religious healing as healing in a genuine state of faith.

A battle with magic weapons between two "ghost-shooters" for the life of a man can hardly be called a religious battle, it seems to me, or the suggestive power of such combatants a religious influence. There may be more of a numinous experience involved when the illness is due to the infraction of a taboo, and the healing to a magic reconciliation with the guardians of the taboo. Yet the substance of the event here too is magical and not religious, even though religious feelings may accompany it. Again, it is natural and not re-

ligious healing that Herophilus has in mind when he
says that medical drugs are the hands of the gods, although the accompanying interpretation is expressed
in religious terms. We may compare this with a statement of Hiltner's today, which says: "All healing
comes from the *vis medicatrix naturae* or the *vis medicatrix Dei*, the healing power of nature or of God,
depending upon whether we are making an empirical
or a religious statement." But to derive magical and
scientific healing from the Ultimate is not to produce
a case of religious healing. And a religious statement
about healing is not, *ipso facto*, a statement about religious healing.

We make a sharp distinction between magic and
religion. Magic is "a universal attitude toward the universe." [2] "It was primitive man's philosophy. It was his
attitude toward nature. Everybody was a magician." [3]
Magic was not only theory, however, it was also a
technical method of dealing with natural objects, including men. It was a world-view, not a religion.
Magic healing is in itself no more religious than physical healing; it is an art, a technique, presupposing a
theory about the causes of illness.

The essence of this theory of magic can be described
as *the belief in a sympathetic interdependence of all
parts of the universe*. This definition, of course, presupposes a high degree of abstraction, and did not appear before the development of rational philosophy.

But the existence of the belief itself is as old as the known history of mankind. The definition is derived from the world-view of the later Stoics, for instance, Poseidonios, for whom the universe is a single living whole in which every part is related to every other part in such a way that it can indicate the state of the other part and of the whole. In this way one can speak of a "cosmic symptomology": everything is a symptom of the state of everything else. . . .

It seems to me most important for the whole problem of religion and health to recognize that the magical world-view is not religion, no more or less so than is the physical world-view. It was in the name of religion, as well as of science, that Robert Boyle fought against the Hippocratean "physics" and the Paracelsian "archaeus" as idols set up between God and the world. The word "nature," which before Leibnitz and Kant had magical connotations, should be replaced, he said, by the word "mechanism" coined by Boyle himself. God made the world as a mechanism of great perfection but without a power of its own. This synthesis of a Calvinistic and a Cartesian attitude toward nature shows that religion can accept a scientific world-view as well as a magical one. Religion is not magic, and magic is not religion. *Religion is the relation to something ultimate, unconditioned, transcendent.* The religious attitude is consciousness of *dependence* (cf. Schleiermacher's unconditional dependence), *surrender* (cf. Eckhard's *Entwerdung*, mystical annihilation, or Calvin's absolute obedience), *acceptance* (cf. Luther's taking, not giving, as first in religion). It concerns the whole man, is person-centered and ethical.

Stated in this way, the distinction between religion and magic is a clear and simple one. Magic is a special kind of interrelation between finite powers; religion is the human relation to the infinite power and value. Magic can be creative and destructive, while religion stands essentially against the destructive powers. Magic is the exercise of immanent power, religion is the subjection to the transcendent power, and so on. But these differences are clearly visible only on the basis of a religious development in which prophetic or mystical criticism has definitely established the unconditional character of the Unconditioned, or the ultimate character of the Ultimate. And even then, the distinction is permanently endangered from two sides. First, there is the necessity that the transcendent manifests itself concretely, and, thereupon, these concrete manifestations become for the religious imagination magic powers. And second, there is the natural desire of man to gain power over the divine, thus making it an object of magical practices.

The divine beings or gods are the most important example of the first danger. They are bearers of the Ultimate in being and in what ought to be, the two sides of every religion. But they are, at the same time, "powers," whose plurality indicates that none of them is really ultimate. Thus, they represent religious meaning, but in magic terms. The prophetic, as well as the mystical, battle against so-called polytheism was the world-historical way of liberating religion from identification with magic. But this battle can never come to an end, for the necessary ambiguity of every image of the divine is a permanent problem of religion, philosophy, and theory of man.

On the subjective side, if dreams and visions of a typically psychic character play the role of means of religious revelation, then the spiritual is experienced in the form of the psychic. Hence, religion must pay continuous attention to the criteria of revelatory experiences. If they belong only to the universe of sympathy, which is the psychic universe, they cannot be considered revelations in the religious sense. But if, in spite of having the general structure of magical sympathy, they are the bearers of *an ultimate, unconditioned concern*, then they are religious. Spiritualistic movements and their assumed revelations keep the necessity of a criterion very urgently before both theology and psychology.

Examples of the second danger to a true concept of religion, arising from the human attempt to gain a magical influence over the divine powers, are abundant. The magical distortion of prayer, from a form of union with the Ultimate symbolized as divine will or divine ground, into a form of using higher powers for personal purposes, is not only one of the most obvious phenomena in the history of religion, but it is a continuous temptation in every high religion, and every Christian minister can witness to it. The form of prayer necessarily has this ambiguity, which cannot lead religion, however, to the dropping of this form, as some radical Protestant theologians are inclined to do, but only to a continuous attention to the danger of confusing the magical and the religious.

Equally refined is the amalgamation of these two in the sacramental sphere. The Reformers attacked the magical distortion of the sacraments in the Roman church. For them the idea that the sacraments have an effect beyond the conscious center of the personality through their mere performance (*opus operatum*) was magic. Instead of it, they demanded the "word" which appeals to consciousness and evokes man's answer in a personal decision. Thereby they left to Protestant theology the practically unsolved problem of the meaning of the sacraments.

The examples show that, while the distinction between religion and magic is logically unambiguous, in reality there is always a certain ambiguity to be overcome. But the last example can help us to make still another step. The tension between a religion of the word and a religion of the sacrament indicates a polarity in the nature of religion itself. Indeed, exclusive emphasis on the person-centered pole in Protestantism and some types of Judaism, found opposition, not only from the Catholic and semi-Catholic side, but also from within these groups themselves. Schleiermacher's definition of religion as a kind of feeling, rightly interpreted by Rudolf Otto as "numinous" experience, was one inroad from the other pole within Protestantism. Others are seen in movements for liturgical reform and for religious healing. It appears very significant that according to Professor Murray of Harvard, "the tendency to form complexes is on the average most frequent in Jews, Protestants occupying the second place, and Catholics only the third." [4]

A widespread interpretation of magic holds it to be true in principle in so far as it is based on "suggestion," perhaps including telepathy. This assumption has weight because it would explain a great deal of the effectiveness of magical practices, especially in the realm of healing. It is important to note that this explanation involves re-establishing a sphere in which man is neither man nor body in the Cartesian sense, but something intermediate. "To suggest" (that is, to bring under the skin, to wit, into the unconscious) has a double meaning. On the one hand, it designates a hint, an insinuation, a proposal whereby the freedom of him who receives the suggestion is preserved. On the other hand, it designates the introduction or stimulation of an idea or impulse in somebody whereby his freedom is disregarded. The second concept is the important one for our problem, but in many, perhaps in most cases, there is no sharp boundary line between the two meanings. A suggested idea is accepted with the help of the suggestive power of somebody.

According to Myers, suggestion can be defined as "the process of effectively impressing upon the subliminal intelligence the wishes of a man's own supraliminal self or that of some other person." The concept of "magnetism," used by Paracelsus and Mesmer, points to the same thing that Maxwell recommended as sympathetic cure by external and internal suggestion. From the temple incubation at the Asklepian center in Kos to the miraculous cures of Our Lady of Lourdes, suggestion, through dreams, visions, and religious faith, has played an important part. Dawson sums up his ideas in this statement: "The entire outlook on life may be altered by the practice of religious suggestions, especially autosuggestions."

But, beyond both of these forms of suggestion, the highest healing power is that of faith, because this involves the spiritual center of man. The ambiguity of the whole situation is thus indicated, for the magical and the religious spheres are again seen to merge in what is called "religious suggestion." Yet Hiltner is right in stressing that genuine religious healing is not by suggestion. We must ask, however, is it without suggestion? I myself do not believe that this is ever possible. For, besides the conscious acceptance of an idea or a demand, elements of the situation always sink into the unconscious and have effects. The suggestive power of a Catholic mass in a medieval cathedral, or of a revivalist in a denominational camp meeting, or a minister alongside a sickbed are realities which can not be denied or removed by religious purism. But the question must be raised whether the elements which grasp the unconscious are bearers of the Ultimate, and whether they are received by the total personality instead of remaining strange bodies within it.

By holding on to this question a decision can be given concerning the relation of healing by suggestion and healing by faith. But, first, it is necessary to liberate the word "faith" from all inferior connotations (for example, as opinion without much evidence, or acceptance of authorities on irrational grounds, or subjection to foreign or autosuggestion), and to restore it to its true religious sense, in which faith is the state of being grasped by the Ultimate. Then we can say that healing in the spiritual or genuine religious sense is mediated by faith. And this act of being made whole in relation to the ultimate ground and meaning of our existence influences all sides of our personality in the direction of wholeness, psyche, mind, and body.

But the term "faith-healing" becomes inappropriate for such an event, for it is ordinarily used for cases of an evidently suggestive character; and healing with religious material through suggestion is not religious healing in the sense just indicated. In every case it is necessary to ask how faith and suggestion are related to each other. The suggested material may appear in an act of genuine faith, or it may not. And, likewise, healing through autosuggestion with religious ideas may be an occasion for faith, or, again, a factor working against real faith.

In the course of this discussion, a certain number of problems have shown themselves, and for some of them solutions have been suggested. But the basic question still remains: What is the structural relation of the "middle sphere" of human nature, the "psychic" reality, to the spiritual and bodily realities? If this is answered (provisionally, of course, as in any other scientific answer), the relations of the various ways of healing to each other can be derived from it.

It may be helpful here to make use of a model already referred to, which shows the mutual relations of the bodily, psychic, and mental spheres. This model, of which some elements were first conceived by Plotinus, in our context has no more significance than a model in physics or chemistry; it merely simplifies for descriptive purposes things which in reality are infinitely more complex.

It may be said in a mythical symbol, that psyche turns one face toward mind and another toward body, and that in the same way, body turns one face toward psyche and another toward *physis*, while the mind turns one face toward psyche and another toward reason. This indicates that in body as well as in mind, there is something intimately united with the psychic sphere, and something alien to it and only indirectly united with it. The former assertion is an acceptance of the belief that man is a dynamic unity, while the latter makes it clear how the understanding of man as a static composite could have been developed successfully.

First, however, we must ask the question: What, in the light of our model, is the nature of the bodily or the biological sphere—life in the sense of living beings? Is the life process merely a complex physico-chemical mechanism whose perfection and duration can be enhanced by physical and chemical repairs? Or are the physical and chemical structures used by a "plan," an "entelechy," a "life principle" (which, of course, is not a causality along with others, but the direction in which the causes are effective)? In the first case, bodily medicine alone would suffice; neither from the psychic nor from the mental side could healing influences be expected. In the second case, influencing and strengthening the living organism as a whole would direct the course of physico-chemical causality, and might produce healing effects.

The age-old idea of the *vis medicatrix naturae* is in agreement with this presupposition. But the question is, what is this totality of causal chains which is "centered" or "directed" without the aid of an additional causality? The "ontological compulsion" always to apply the causal scheme, even where we must prohibit its use, may prevent us from ever gaining an insight into the nature of a life-centered causality. But, however we describe this structure, the center is not omnipotent, and the body is turned with one face toward *physis*, the physico-chemical realm, open to its influences, in disorder, disintegration, and healing. This is the justification for the relative independence of purely medical methods and the "anatomic pattern" despite criticism from all kinds of "natural healing."

The second question refers to the relationship of the psychic element to the rational element in the nature of the mind. Reason, in the classical sense, is the system of categories, structures, and universals, which have practical and theoretical validity (however the ontological nature of this validity and the possibility of knowing it, is thought of). In each of its acts the mind is related to the reasonable structure of reality, but in such a way that it drives beyond any special element, and even beyond the universe itself, toward the ultimate ground and meaning of the whole and the special forms within it. This "driving beyond" in asking and receiving is what we mean by religion.

The mind is directed toward the valid norms and structures of reality (the Scholastics called this *intentionalitas*, directedness toward the objectively valid) as the mathematician's mind is directed toward valid equations. But the mind is also directed toward the bearer of intentionality, the psyche with its striving forces, for without these psychic forces no mental act is possible. But even more, the contents of the mental acts are determined, not only by the objective structures of reality, but also by the psychic reception of them. How is this possible? It would be impossible if the mind were something like a logical machine—corresponding to the physical machine of the physico-chemical interpretation of life—guided by clear and distinct insights, and misguided by the lack of perfect perceptions. In this case, the psychic sphere could only be regarded as a disturbing element in the operation of the mind. Mental and spiritual healing would be unthinkable. In so far as the mind is concerned, no healing would be needed, only enlightenment (cf. Kant's demand that the mentally ill be turned over to the philosophers), and, in so far as illness is concerned, it would be purely bodily.

The opposite solution regards the contents of the mind as "sublimations" of psychic drives. But the term sublimation is ambiguous; it can deny the objective validity of the results of sublimation, in which case the "principle of reality" is abandoned, and all the contents of religion and culture are *nothing but* projections of psychic instincts. This is absurd, because it undermines the theory of sublimation as much as any other theory. Or, sublimation may be regarded as the process in which the unconscious drives are united with valid contents, in which case it states the problem of psyche and mind, but does not solve it. Is there any way of formulating the psychic-mental unity?

"Man uses his animal instincts in order to build his loftiest ideals and . . . his loftiest ideals consequently derive their energies from his animal drives, albeit domesticated." This would seem to imply that the instincts are, though in a primitive or undomesticated form, essentially related to the contents of the mind, that is, to religion and culture.

Furthermore, it seems to imply that the rational side of mental questioning derives its creative and dynamic power from a prerational element in the mind, which may be called feeling, affect, passion, emotion (the terminology is very unstable). This prerational element would direct the rational element in a specific direction; thus, religion and culture would be based on a *union of structure and passion*. If this formulation is acceptable (though probably no more understandable than life-centered causality), it would be more than mere poetry to say, in the spirit of St. Augustine, that the drives originating in the psyche are restless until they find rest in union with the mind. And mental healing would be the art of helping this union come to pass by guiding the psychic forces in that direction in which, by their very nature, they want to go in order to find rest.

There is something in the structure of mind and reality which transcends itself, not toward another, higher realm, but toward a special qualification of both the prerational and rational elements, namely, the spiritual. The spiritual is not a sphere outside the mind, as the Unconditioned is not a reality outside the conditioned, nor the Ultimate a stage above the preliminary. The spiritual is a qualification of the mind, the Unconditioned is a dimension of the conditioned, and the Ultimate is the point of reference for everything preliminary. All creations of the mind have such a spiritual element, in so far as they have an ultimate meaning and significance. Therefore, any attempt to guide the psychic drives must take into consideration not only the mental contents as such, but also their hidden or manifest spiritual qualification.

Spiritual healing is the depth-dimension of mental healing; it is potentially, if not actually, present, whether it expresses itself in the seriousness and profundity of the psychotherapeutic situation, or in explicit religious manifestations. However, it is also true that mental healing—and through it bodily healing—is a potential, though not always actual, consequence of spiritual healing, whether an intentional one, as in religious counseling, or unintentionally produced by preaching and liturgy. These distinctions should prevent a confusion of functions: the spirituality of a psychiatric situation is not dependent on any religious reference; nor is the psychic power of a religious situation dependent on any psychiatric reference.

And now we must introduce a great simplification of our model. We must say that the face the psyche turns toward the body, and the face the body turns toward the psyche, constitute a common sphere; and that the face the psyche turns toward the mind, and the face the mind turns toward the psyche, also constitute a common sphere. The vital and the unconscious drives are the same, seen from two sides; and the prerational process of the mind and the conscious process of the psyche are the same, seen from two sides. The latter statement is corroborated by Zilboorg: "A psychological phenomenon is a biological function for which no specialized organ is found in the living organism." "Fear, love, hatred, admiration, sense of guilt and remorse, sense of righteousness and indignation, compassion and contempt—every shade of human emotions" are total functions, and, as such, are the concern of the psychiatrist.

There is, consequently, psychic reality in the body and in the mind, the first, unconscious, the second, conscious, and the question which finally must be answered is: How are these two sides related to each other? The answer, derived from our model, must be: The unconscious becomes actually what it potentially is, and for which it strives, by reaching the state of consciousness; and the consciousness includes the potentialities driving within the unconscious as its vital reservoir. Potentiality is not actuality, but neither is it nothing; it is *potentia*, power; the most destructive power, if it conquers the mental unity of consciousness after having been repressed; the most creative power, if it enters and widens the consciousness through union with the objective structures of reality.

The success of this union determines the integration (or disintegration) of the personality; it decides between disease and health, and between destruction and salvation.

FOOTNOTES

1. From a paper delivered at the Seminar on Religion and Health of the Columbia University Seminars on Religion, 1945-46. Reprinted by permission of "The Review of Religion."

2. Lynn Thorndike, *The Place of Magic in the Intellectual History of Europe* (New York: Columbia University Press, 1905), p. 34.

3. *Ibid.*, p. 29.

4. Editor's Note: This generalization and its interpretation were disputed in the Seminar discussion as statistically unreliable and ambiguous in probable significance.

Spiritual Healing in the Light of History

Spiritual Cures Cannot Be Explained on the Basis of Psychosomatic Medicine—They Are Much More Far-Reaching in Their Dramatic Character

THE HISTORY of religion in general and of Christianity in particular abundantly witnesses to the fact that spontaneous healings occur within a religious context. Whether we think of the cult of Asklepios, or of primitive Christianity, or of the healing powers of medieval monks and kings, or of the Reformation or of the rise of Methodism, or of Christian Science or of modern Lourdes, we are confronted with overwhelming testimony to remarkable cures. However much, moreover, we may discount earlier records, the patient researches of the *Bureau des Constatations medicales*, at Lourdes, make us aware that such things happen in our own day.

206

People are cured of a wide range of physical sick-
nesses without the aid of medical or surgical methods.
Pulmonary tuberculosis, paralysis, rheumatism, frac-
tures, ulcers, and cancer have been permanently healed.
Of that there can now be no doubt. Nor would we
be wise to try to explain such cures on the basis of
psychosomatic medicine. They are much more far-
reaching in their dramatic character. Just as many
medical authorities were in error a half a century ago
when they denied the existence of such cures, so we
now should be in error were we to resolve them solely
into psychosomatic terms.

The new understanding of the interrelations between physical well-being and the emotions, is insufficient to account for them fully. They surpass what
psychosomatic medicine ever has done. We can learn,
indeed, from psychosomatics a hint of what is involved, but only a hint. The religious factor is more
primary.

It was not accidental, furthermore, that Christianity
should, from the start, have appeared as a healing cult.
Against the Greek disparagement of the body, the
Christian affirmed its resurrection, and thought of salvation in terms of the healing of the *whole* person—
body, mind, and spirit. Salvation meant the recovery
of wholeness or holiness, for these words (and their
Greek counterparts) are originally identical in meaning and derived from the same roots. Hence the
Saviour was at the same time the Healer—a point

which the opening chapter of Mark's Gospel makes
with great clarity.

Spiritual cures have certain *marked characteristics*
which tend to recur in all the accounts, be they the
records of Epidauros or of Lourdes. There is often a
sudden acute pain which is directly related to the
cure. There is the lack of a time factor. The healing
is sudden, with no intervening period of convales-
cence. There is permanence. There is an ambiguous
relation between faith and doubt, though faith in some
form (of the patient, or the healer, or the church) is
invariably present. There is a general atmosphere of
religious expectation. And finally such cures are re-
markably infrequent. About one per cent (or less) of
the pilgrims to Lourdes receive bodily healing.

Spiritual healing, furthermore, is of two different
types which need to be distinguished. First there is
charismatic healing, where the healer himself plays the
primary role. He possesses the "gift of healing" recognized in the New Testament (I Corinthians 12:28)
and in the Early Church. Such healers form a rather
definite type. Origen early remarked, "For the most
part it is the uneducated who do these things. . . . The
overcoming of demons is not in need of anyone wise
or powerful in the rational demonstration of the faith."
(*Contra Celsum*, 7:4) That is to say, such persons are
generally those in whom the critical spirit is less developed, and who are of the visionary or "psychic"

type. Certain rigorous disciplines, moreover, such as prolonged fasting and celibacy, seem also related to their success.

Then again, such healers often have definite and limited areas in which their work is effective. Far more study has to be done before we can probe the matter more deeply. We may note, however, that the disrepute into which spiritual healing has often fallen, has not a little to do with the fact that such healers are generally of a nonrational type, given to romanticizing their cures and living in a semisymbolic realm in which faith tends to supplant knowledge. Their records are so often inaccurate, and their willingness to encounter critical appraisal often so lacking, that the study of their work is indeed difficult.

But though we must recognize this, we must not fall into the error of supposing that all their reported cures are fiction. The fact seems to be that the development of the critical spirit *hinders* this type of work, and is a real danger to the religious healer. (We meet precisely the same situation in the study of para-normal psychology. The strange powers of genuine mediums are notoriously hard to assess, since a critical atmosphere hinders their operation.) Yet the genuine nature of such healings must not be waved aside for this reason. Those who are able to appraise the material most fruitfully, are exactly the people who are least able to do the cures themselves. Rather should they rejoice that there *are* such people in the world, and accept the limitations under which religious healers have to work.

The other type of religious healing is *sacramental*. It depends for its efficiency upon the power of religious tradition and the faith of the Church. Not the charismatic individual, but the sacramental form is of primary importance. The laying on of hands and the anointing with oil have, indeed, often been used by charismatics. But here I refer rather to the sacramental rites of the Church, which the ordained minister celebrates. The power of the sacrament does not depend on the faith of the minister or of the patient. It depends on the communal tradition and faith of the Church as a whole, on the general seriousness (or "intention") of the clergyman and on the receptivity (rather than the active faith) of the patient. This last point is very important. A sick patient should not be urged to screw himself up to a pitch of faith and expectation. Rather should he be led to open himself to the gift of God which comes *as a gift* through the ministry of the Church.

It is not possible here to develop the long history of Holy Unction, but two points may be noted. As a New Testament sacrament (Mark 6:13, James 5:14-16) it was originally (as in Judaism) *a healing rite*. And it was naturally closely associated with confession of sins, since the relation of sin to sickness (though not so direct as the Reformers imagined) is inseparable. Right relations with God depend upon confession, and the reception of God's gifts is impossible without it. Sickness is the consequence of sin, and Satan not God is its author (Luke 13:16). But a particular sickness cannot necessarily be directly associated with a particular sin. Rather is sickness one of the ways in which original sin expresses itself and holds captive the human race.

The other point about Holy Unction concerns its decline as a healing rite and its transformation into a preparation for death. This came about through the patristic revival in the Carolingian Renaissance. There occurred a restoration of the rite which had become increasingly disused. But the restoration meant reinterpretation. The number of healings had become so small that the rite was given a general spiritual meaning, and became finally "Extreme Unction," a preparation for death, in which the anticipation of bodily healing was secondary. The original healing emphasis of the liturgy was transformed into one of forgiveness of sins. Nowadays (in both Catholic and Protestant circles) there is a return to the more primitive meaning, though this has a corresponding danger that only bodily healing should be associated with rite.

This, indeed, is a fundamental danger in all spiritual healing, and one into which the more widely advertised spiritual healers of our day constantly fall. There is nothing more tragic than to witness the disappointment of those who set their whole hope on being healed at some spectacular service, and go away empty. Or the disappointment of those who, in some emotional trauma, find themselves able to throw away their crutches only to discover quickly afterward that their last state is worse than their first. This is the degradation of spiritual healing, for it misunderstands its whole meaning.

What then shall we say of *spiritual healing?*

First that, in the experience of the Church, it is *extremely rare*. Over against Christian Science and healing sects, we must be sober and realize that medicine cures more often and more surely than the charismatic healer or Holy Unction.

But, second, we must not forget that spiritual healing, though rare, is *very real*. When it comes, it can come with a dramatic suddenness and spectacular character which far outdistance modern medicine. That is why *we must always provide the occasion for it*. Here ministers have often been most lax, either from disbelief or from ignorance. By prayer or unction, or with the help of the charismatic healer, we are in duty bound to set the stage, as it were, through which the Spirit of God *may* operate. It is God and not we who does the healing; but without our prayers and sacraments, the channels of his grace may be wanting. We must not raise false hopes; neither must we quench the Spirit. When right relations with God are established through confession of sins and thanksgiving, who can say if the Spirit will not raise up the sick man? We wait on the Spirit of God, earnestly believing that he works with power. The issue is in his hands, who creates and redeems according to his good pleasure. The miracle may come through our unworthy hands, if we earnestly prepare for it, neither disbelieving nor being overanxious. For it is not bodily health which is of supreme importance, but right relations with God.

Ultimately we all die, and sickness, the consequence of sin, overcomes us all, till in the resurrection we are made one with Christ. This tragic element in mortal existence must be the background against which we understand spiritual healing. It is a *token* of the Resurrection, an instance of the way in which the Church participates even now in the Kingdom. It is an aspect of realized eschatology. But just as the Church is not yet the Kingdom, but only a foreshadowing of it, and just as we now possess the Spirit, but only as a token or "earnest" of a future inheritance, so the miracle of healing is but a breaking through of powers to be realized in the future, when death shall be swallowed up in victory.

So when we approach the bedside of the sick, let us pray earnestly for healing, let us bring the New Testament sacrament of Unction, let us tell the stories of Jesus' miracles, as did the ancient liturgies for the visitation of the sick. Let us wait upon God with faith and expectation; but let us not be overanxious for the things of this world. We can serve God in health, but sometimes even more through the mystery of sickness, whose redemption lies deeper than merely being rid of it. It lies in the redemption of sin of which sickness is an outward token of the disruption of created nature.

This final victory, accomplished in the Christ, lies at the end of history. We participate in it by anticipation in the Church, but only by anticipation. Sometimes the powers of the life to come break in upon our mortal existence and point us toward that End to which we move in Christ. But these are but transitory tokens of what is not yet fulfilled. To claim more for spiritual healing than that is to beguile the innocent and to sow the seeds of tragedy darker than sickness itself. It is to raise false hopes and to teach men to put their faith in the body rather than in Christ.

It may be well, finally, to ask in what sense spontaneous healings can be called *miracles*. Let us begin by realizing that such healings occur outside as well as within a religious context. The charismatic healer, moreover, is not always a religious man. Like every mortal gift, religion has no monopoly of this kind of healing. Spontaneous cures occur within many different contexts and are undoubtedly related to that mysterious *psi* element in human nature, which modern para-psychology posits to explain such powers as extrasensory perception and so on. What makes such cures "spiritual" is their religious relationship. That gives them the character of miracles.

Now a miracle is not the changing of a predetermined course of nature by an arbitrary God. Rather is it the emergence of latent, creative powers within a religious context. Miracles are both "signs" and "powers" (to use the New Testament words): signs because they point to God; powers because of their unusual and dynamic character. It is by virtue of the latter that they are able to point to God. Their surprising nature symbolizes his Otherness.

Not every spontaneous cure therefore, is a miracle; but only those which are seen to disclose God, which awaken faith and which reveal, rather than obscure, the Creator behind his works. Miracles are translucent of the Divine; for they direct the attention not to themselves, but beyond themselves to their Source. They have a "natural" explanation, in the sense that they belong to the created order and follow its patterns. As we have said, spontaneous healings are related to the *psi* factor in our nature. But what makes them miracles is not that they happen, but that they have the transparent quality of revealing God.

The close connection between religious disciplines and the *psi* factor is one of the things which the history of religion amply demonstrates, and which invites much more serious study than it has yet received. The element of the miraculous in ancient and medieval religion has often enough not been taken seriously. But when we see it in this light, as the emergence of creative powers in a religious context, much that was formerly dark and discredited, becomes illuminated. Miracles do not dispense with the order of created nature. They are that part of nature through which the religious man can most easily detect the Divine.

When, then, we pray for the miracle of religious healing, we do not pray for something beyond the order of nature, but for the emergence of creative powers which as much belong to that order as any other. It is no more "natural" for a disease to pursue its usual course, than for it to eventuate in spontaneous healing. The difference lies in the kind of natural powers that are brought to bear on the situation. It is no more "natural" (though certainly more usual) for me to learn what is in my wife's mind by her telling me directly, than for me to sense it through telepathy. They are just two different ways in which the created order works.

Science and Spiritual Healing

The Basic Principle of Spiritual Healing Is the Recognition of Powers Which Transcend Those of the Human Mind

IN THE COURSE of the last thirty years an increasing number of physicians and laymen have accepted the concept that illness of mind and body can be caused by psychological influences and that they can be treated successfully by psychologic methods. Much of this development is recognized nowadays as scientifically well founded because the findings satisfied two crucial criteria: they occurred often enough to be *statistically significant* and the observations could be *repeated experimentally* in hospital or laboratory. "Spiritual healing" cannot expect to be recognized on the same basis: it does not occur often enough to satisfy the statisticians and it cannot be produced deliberately either by renowned healers or by visits to Lourdes and similar places. Even more inacceptable to

most scientists is the claim that healing can be effecte
without direct contact with the patient as this i
claimed for intercessory prayer and for many indi
vidual healers. The existence of such cases is eithe
ignored or explained as due to coincidence, the vener
able *deus ex machina* of old and new fiction.

The negative attitude of the majority of contem
porary scientists and educated laymen should not b
taken for a scientific verdict that spiritual healing i
impossible. Its two main features, unusual behavior o
matter and communication without physical mean
of transmission, have been proved possible accordin
to the most exacting standards of science. The reason
for skepticism regarding such cures will be discusse
after the theoretical foundations of miraculous cure
have been examined.

As to the concept of *matter* on which we base ou
everyday actions, its apparent solidity has been prove
an illusion of our sense organs. It comes about in
manner roughly similar to the illusion of solid object
in three-dimensional moving pictures: as a result o
electronic processes which take place in practicall
empty space. The space occupied at any given mo
ment by electrons is less than the billionth part of th
most solid object perceived by our senses so that th
"material" part of our body could be contained in a
little space as occupied by a droplet of water. No
only is the solidity of the body an illusion, but als
that the electronic pattern behind it is maintained b

igid laws of nature. Careful observation of individual toms has proved that the electrons composing them ehave in a completely unpredictable manner. In large umbers of atoms only we find the regularities which ave impressed physicists until the beginning of the resent century as immutable laws of nature.

This type of orderliness found in large numbers is f the same character as the constant density of the rowd streaming each weekday from a certain com- nuters' train. Some of the individuals composing this rowd are different from one day to the next due to ersonal circumstances, like oversleeping, illness, vaca- ions, but these varieties of individuals cancel each ther out so that the railroad company can organize s services accordingly. There is, however, no immu- able law of nature why the usually crowded train hould not run empty on a certain day because by co- ncidence all the expected passengers had for different ersonal reasons failed to use this train. Similarly the hysicists assure us that no law of nature would be iolated if, for instance, this magazine before you hould suddenly fall out of your sight. Accidentally ll the electrons composing it could have moved into pattern allowing it to fall through the empty spaces omposing your hand or desk like salt running through he top of a salt shaker. The probability of such an vent is small, but by no means infinitesimal. It can be lefined by a scientifically respectable mathematical

formula. All this has been described by Eddington in
his classic *The Nature of the Physical World* twenty-
five years ago and may be considered a reliable account.

Applying the foregoing, for instance, to the miraculous disappearance of a cancer, such an event does not
contradict the medical experience that the overwhelming majority of cancers spontaneously grow until
they have destroyed the life of the organism. Medicine
has known for some time that "spontaneous cures"
of cancer do occur, but so far scientists have not in-
vestigated the circumstances under which they took
place. At the present time such research is under way.
It suggests that spiritual healing fits into the general
concept developed by psychosomatic medicine: that
bodily diseases express specific psychological conditions of the patient and that they disappear if the underlying condition has disappeared spontaneously or
by treatment.

Spiritual healing agrees with psychosomatic medicine in its recognition that there is a meaningful connection between illness and the psychology of the
patient; it also agrees with the experiences of medical
psychotherapy regarding the importance of the total
individual situation. Unlike routine surgery and drug
medicine, the personalities of the healer and the healed
play an important role for the outcome of the treatment: the most expert hypnotist cannot force the
hypnotized person to do anything violating his con-

science, nor can each expert pyschoanalyst analyze successfully any curable patient. It seems only reasonable to assume that spiritual values are part of the factors affecting therapy. In the course of the last sixteen years the work of Szondi has clarified some of the deeper psychological values which direct and limit all significant human relationships such as the encounter of healer and healed. These findings have been verified by different methods so that they can be considered as scientifically established. They are likely to throw further light on the selective character of spiritual healings.

The second aspect of the phenomenon arousing skepticism is the claim that a person can be cured without being conscious that healing efforts are made in his behalf. The existence of so-called telepathic rapport has been firmly established by many methods: the meticulous case work of the members of the British and American Societies for Psychical Research, the experimental work of Rhine at Duke University,[1] and the work of psychoanalysts who could demonstrate that telepathic rapport takes place under specific psychological conditions of the patient, the physician, and other persons.

As it appears from the preceding statements, neither the unusual physical changes nor the unusual forms of communication found in spiritual healing are incompatible with our scientific knowledge of physics and

of psychology. To explain the resistance against th
acceptance of these phenomena one must consid
their practical and psychological implications. From
practical point of view it is evident that no spiritu
healer and no spiritual healing center, such as Lourde
has accomplished cures frequently enough to warra
the substitution of spiritual healing for the curre
methods of orthodox medicine. Almost all physicia
have encountered sad cases of a curable disease becom
ing fatal while under some form of spiritual treatmen
As our systems of public welfare proceed on a stati
tical basis, spiritual healing cannot be advocated as
substitute for medical healing, but only as part o
therapy. The psychological reason for the gener
skepticism regarding spiritual healing is more signif
cant, however.

Medical healing, as commonly practiced, is base
on a materialistic and anthropocentric concept of th
world. Until Planck and Einstein revolutioniz
physics fifty years ago Western scientists had be
convinced that everything in the material world fo
lowed strict deterministic laws, that same causes pr
duced the same effects and that the scientific physici
of the future would be able to cure each illness b
applying a specific remedy. Originally even psych
analytic therapy was conceived of in a similar mech
nistic fashion: bad psychological influences had pr
duced bad psychological conditions; the psychoan
lyst substituted good influences which should produ

ood psychological conditions. In the classical scheme f therapy the ideal physician changes the world by oplying the "laws" of biology, psychology, and economics to all medical problems. This role of the scintific magician has been so flattering to Western phycians and scientists that most of them are still clinging to it, although it is scientifically untenable.

In this unrealistic faith the medical profession is rengthened by the hypnotic effect of public demands. The increasing spiritual insecurity of modern man has ade him more and more dependent on bodily and conomic security. He has concentrated on the prongation of life and the raising of economic standards illness and deprivation are no longer the acceptable ice of spiritual pursuits. News about "wonder ugs," "miracle cures," "magic bullets," "psychorgery," and so on are therefore a favorite staple of urnalists and publishers. Even religious best sellers, eir titles notwithstanding, have attracted their public often by the promise of material advantages to be rived from religious practice.

At the present time the beneficial power of science s become clearly recognizable as subject to serious nitations. Its wonders appear most convincingly in all areas of life, because they are based on the strict usality which is observable only under ideal laboratory conditions. In perfecting the magic of the laboratory, man turned his back on the wider implications of hat he was doing. The men, for instance, who bom-

barded the atom with electrons were motivated by th
search for the truth about the structure of matter
Nothing destructive seemed to be involved in bring
ing force to bear on isolated atoms in a scientific ap
paratus. Yet the psychological observer realizes tha
the striving of the human will for the mastery of hi
environment is the same in the scientist bombarding a
individual atom, and the statesman who decides t
launch an atomic attack on the capital of an individua
nation. The ethics motivating scientific and political
aggression, respectively, may be of a different order
but it is not an irrational accident that the scientist
wielding destructive powers against atoms produce
also destructive weapons against men.

This may serve as an example for the unforeseeabl
consequences of scientific research and the practica
consequences of the ethos which animates the scien
tists, in this case the devotion to the advancement c
the human mind. Obviously, it can serve constructiv
purposes as well, for instance, the cure of cance
peaceful industries, and so on, but it must be recog
nized that the most basic principle of modern scienc
is based on the faith that man knows good and evi
and that he is the ultimate authority on the use of h
powers. Contrary to current scientific therapy th
basic principle of spiritual healing is the recognitio
of powers which transcend those of the human min

Here the cure depends on values which cannot be made by man, but which must be accepted.

Spiritual healing has never claimed that it can be taught like hypnosis or psychoanalysis. Individual healers consider their power as a "gift," a "charisma" which they may attribute to an accident of nature or to the will of God. In the case of holy places and religious rites the recognition of the superhuman power is explicit. This feature of spiritual healing is naturally offensive to all scientists who cling to the ideal of "man for himself" and his future as the master of the earth, if not of the universe. It produces an emotional resistance which is enforced by the spectacle of irresponsible quacks who exploit real or pretended healing power for personal gain. This, unfortunately, is one of the great moral hazards to which so many individuals and sects have succumbed.

From the point of view of medicine the only rational attitude toward spiritual healing is the recognition that the outcome of an illness depends on influences not subject to will. This insight is an addition to the general progress of our medical knowledge, which has been proceeding from the immediately observable to features which revealed themselves only to more comprehensive and abstract investigations. In the case of tuberculosis, for example, we see nowadays that the inflamed spot of lung around the Koch bacilli is only the most visible result of a vast number of less obvious, though equally indispensable conditions such as the general state of health of the patient at the time he encountered a pathogenic number of virulent bacilli. Underlying this encounter we have to consider the hereditary disposition of the individual, the quality of his emotional relationships, his socio-economic situation, and so on. Just as the top point of a pyramid is most striking and most widely seen only thanks to mostly invisible stone masses underneath, so the spot of the lung visible in the X ray and under the microscope exists only due to more or less invisible factors just enumerated. The spiritual condition of the patient becomes now evident as an additional factor which governs appearance and disappearance of a sick spot of the body. This discovery does not come as a surprise to those who followed the evolution of psychoanalysis and of psychosomatic medicine with an open mind, not to mention those adhering to a religious faith.

The preceding facts and considerations lead to the conclusion that the medical treatment of illness includes concern with the spiritual condition of the patient. No examination of a patient is complete in which the physician has not evaluated the possibility that this sphere requires special religious attention. As so many a patient nowadays has little or no conscious awareness of his spiritual side, the physician cannot always do anything about this aspect of the illness, even where he recognizes it, just as he is often aware of unhealthy family conditions without seeing an opening for psychotherapy. It is evident, however, that spiritual influences are underlying all the therapeutic methods recognized by scientific medicine. They must be considered when we try to explain why some patients die unexpectedly although all the material and psychological conditions made the prognosis favorable, why "hopeless" cases sometimes recover against all scientifically established odds.

The recognition of spiritual healing does not make other therapeutic methods obsolete. One can hardly deny that the more common and therefore better known processes of physics, biology, and psychology are all parts of divine creation. The cases of miraculous healing, not involving biological and psychological agents, appear as more direct expressions of the spiritual relationship between God and the individual. This relationship is not outside of man's scientific endeavors. Spiritual healing reminds us that the old concept of the four faculties of the medieval university had its justification. We cannot hope to understand man fully through the methods of medicine, philosophy, and law alone; we need theology too. This type of scientific approach brings us back to the real meaning of science: knowledge.

It has been one of the unfortunate consequences of the mechanistic era of physics that it was considered the main criterion of scientific progress that it permitted prediction and conscious manipulation of the future. This arrogant misunderstanding of science left no place for the spiritual element in medicine. The scientist who has faced the tremendous depths and powers in the unconscious part of the soul will recognize that healing means not only the fighting of evil forces, but also humble accepting of powers which surpass human ingenuity. Scientific research into the nature of spiritual healing is likely to add to our insights into the meaning of illness and health.

FOOTNOTE

1. J. B. Rhine, *New World of the Mind* (New York: William Sloane Associates, 1954).

WAYNE E. OATES

Pastoral Psychology and Faith Healing

*The Main Task of the Pastoral Psychologist Is
to Develop Methods of Spiritual Healing
Together with Theoretical and
Theological Criteria by Which
to Judge the Soundness
of His Methods*

PERSONAL RELIGION in its full flower, unencumbered by the negative afterthoughts of a tired civilization, usually draws a straight line of connection between faith and health. No amount of exegetical casuistry can remove the practice of faith healing from the center of the reality of the person and work of Christ. Only a wish not to see it can blind one to the continuous constellations of faith healing groups that have formed among Christians from the beginning of the Christian era until now. Only an ivory tower existence can insulate one from the knowledge of the variety of healing groups among Christians today. Careful confrontation of the salient issues at stake in the practice of faith healing is in order for those who engage in the practice of pastoral psychology. What are some of the psychological issues at stake in faith healing?

A. The first issue at stake is the essentially charismatic nature of much that is today being given us as "scientific" counseling. Both in the realm of pastoral counseling (and its mainspring of secular psychotherapy) a pastoral psychologist is more and more impressed by the fact that both he and his colleagues depend upon certain personal *gifts* of insight and action when the path of a given counseling relationship becomes a new one, one which has not been traversed before. In order to keep from appearing too pious, we are likely to say: "I followed a hunch here, and it paid off." Only occasionally will we say what we as incurably religious folk feel "deep down." If we did say that, we would likely say: "I moved on faith here. I trusted in the Lord, and he revealed to me which way I should go with this person."

Furthermore, the indescribability of our experience as counselors as we participate in nonverbal levels of communication with counselees makes of our healing work as counselors an intense relationship of faith. As Korzybski has said, we can only "point at" and can never verbalize the ineffable realities with which we grapple day after day in a consistent counseling ministry. The religious person searches for methods of communicating both with himself and others about this in terms of the thought of the great mystics and poetic seers of other days, as well as in the words of novelists and dramatists. The scientific psychologist and/or psychotherapist may develop a clandestine relationship to para-psychology or to the Bhagavad Gita in order to avoid re-examining the original sources of the Christian tradition from which bad religious education and pastoral carelessness have alienated him.

Nevertheless, most counseling still reveals that "X" quality that is "given" and not achieved, felt and not understood, which makes of counseling an art and not a science, an act of faith and not merely of sight. This is the first consideration for the more sophisticated reader of this chapter on "faith healing."

B. The second issue at stake in a consideration of faith healing is an indictment of both trained medical doctors (and there are still too many of them with insufficient training for the social responsibility they are accepting) and of trained ministers. These professionally trained persons have gravitated geographically to the city and away from the rural areas of the world. They have gravitated upward in their social class and away from the lower social classes. As a result, the medical aid and the religious instruction available to the lowest classes of our country, and especially to the rural people, quite regularly consist of the "home remedies" of both medicine and religion. In fact, to put it bluntly, if large segments of people in the areas where I have been pastor get healed, it will be by faith in God alone. Only God and their praying neighbors are really on the job. This fact was true also in the days of the writing of the New and Old Testaments. Few medical resources were available. This intensified the dependence of people upon God (and upon their dietary laws which they perceived to be from God). By the same token such naïve simplifications of life are unencumbered by the pseudophilosophical vagaries of a dyspeptic culture. Likewise, the lack of tangible and demonstrated medical procedures quickened their search for a theological world view that was adequate to take care of them in a day when life was even more uncertain than it is now.

C. A psychosocial observation needs clarification at this point. Neither the professional medical practitioner (without psychiatric orientation) nor the professional religious practitioner has tended to take seriously the complaints of people which do not easily fit their "rule of thumb"; and "quickie" techniques and theories of "what-is-wrong-with-people-and-how-to-get-them-well" protect the doctor and the minister from the risks and rubs involved in a personal encounter with the patient himself. No interpersonal relationships are necessary.

This is illustrated in a report made by a pastor:

"The husband had been one of the wickedest men

in our community. Then during our annual revival in the Methodist Church, he had been gloriously saved. It was truly one of the most genuine conversions I had ever seen. But he had a cross to bear in that his wife, who had before been a very active Christian, began to lose her interest in religion. She quit her offices in the church and soon quit coming to church altogether. Then she became openly critical of him and his 'religious fanaticism.' I really lost patience with her. Instead of being a help to this new convert, she was a stumbling block.

"Then one day while visiting in their home, I spoke to her directly about it. She broke down into tears and told me that before they had moved to our community she had been divorced. He had married her before he became a Christian. Now that he had become a Christian, he felt that he was living in adultery for having married a divorced woman. Therefore, he had decided to keep up the appearances of a happy and religious home, but never to have sexual relations with her at all. This has been going on since his conversion two years ago. She is about wild."

Both the doctor and the minister can be so involved in dispensing their "standardized" solutions to people's problems that they allow the more personal aspects of their ministry to go undone. Such persons as have been mentioned are ready prey for cultic groups that emphasize faith healing, all out of proportion to common sense, intelligent medical practice, or sound religious teaching.

In lower class social groups that tend to be uneducated, economically underprivileged, and religiously unsophisticated, the cultural pattern of thinking is such as to make them naïvely dependent upon authoritarian and hypnotic faith healers who work among them as representatives of the sects. Similarly persons in upper middle classes and upper classes (who nevertheless are given to boredom, a loss of meaning, and who are borne down by emptiness of existence) quite often turn to the sophisticated types of faith healers found in the cults such as Theosophy, New Thought, Unity, and the like. The psychology of social classes has much to teach at this point. A pastor cannot effectively grasp and cope with the needs for his people for health through faith apart from an ordered sociological insight and information.

D. One of the main tasks of a pastoral psychologist is to develop methods of spiritual healing and to develop ethical and theological criteria by which to judge the soundness of his methods as they are developed. The psycho-ethical criteria for distinguishing valid methods of faith healing from spurious ones need clarification.

1. The first way of making this distinction inheres in the kind of answer the healer gives to the fact of death. This lies at the core of the problem of disease and the search for health. Death is the hallmark of

man's finitude, decisive crises, and is thrust upon him in illness. The way in which a faith healer deals with the fact of death is a criterion as to determining whether he is to be trusted wholeheartedly. Faith healers have historically dealt with the fact of death in two ways:

The faith healer who denies, distorts, or glosses over the fact of physical death does his healing on the basis of unreality. The Johannine story of the raising of Lazarus pinpoints this distinction. The disciples wanted to believe that Lazarus' condition was something else other than death. They said that it was sleep, but Jesus is interpreted by the author:

> Now Jesus had spoken of his death, but they thought that he meant taking rest in sleep. Then Jesus told them plainly, "Lazarus is dead" . . . (John 11:13-14)

Further in the narrative, the author underlines this again by referring to the fact of the smell of the decaying body of a person who had been dead four days. (See vv. 38-40.)

Once, however, a faith healer has, on the basis of a barrage of theosophical teaching, convinced the sick person that there is no such thing as death, then he can relax the power of the disease for a season. However, this is the seed-bed of neurosis itself. The needs of the person to feel that he is exempt from death, which is the common lot of humanity, come into action. The disease has not been healed, but has moved from an organic point of concentration to a psychoneurotic center of unreality in thought. Such an unrealistic approach to death itself borders upon sorcery, and as such, is spurious. The dramatic, temporary results of such sorcery are often quite convincing at first. However, such results are dependent upon continued exposure to the influence of the so-called therapist who produces similar results again and again by the repetition of the first procedure.

From a psychological point of view such releases from anxiety and its resultant symptoms are sought by passive-dependent individuals who have a high degree of "extractive eroticism" in their make-up. The repeated incantations of the religious personage tend to be gratification "long-circuits" for otherwise unacceptable and unmanageable erotic impulses.

2. A second and antithetical approach to the fact of death is the realism of the Christian view of death and the practice of counseling. Jesus put it paradoxically when he said: "If any man would come after me, let him deny himself and take up his cross and follow me. For whoever would save his life will lose it, and whoever loses his life for my sake will find it." (Matthew 16:24-25) This passage is set in the context of Jesus' own acceptance of the inevitability of his own death on the cross. Partially following the thought of Schopenhauer, we can say that "death is the price we pay for life." The secret of disease and death lies in birth,

and the secret of health and life lies in the acceptance of death as a reality.

In the context of this realism about death, the fact of Christian cross bearing—that is, the acceptance of the reality of our creatureliness, finitude, and limitation epitomized in the fact of death—cannot be deleted from healing without removing faith from it. Such healing is no longer *faith healing* but is sorcery and magic.

The drama of actual healings in which I have participated were healings for a period of time (for all healing is simply the delaying—not the removal—of the time of death). One person was a forty-five-year-old Baptist minister who was admitted to the hospital (of which I was chaplain) after suffering a heart attack. He spent about three weeks trying "with all his might" to live. He kept getting worse until his doctors felt that he had only a few more hours to live. The man was told by his doctors of the seriousness of his condition. He accepted the fact of his impending death and bade his family farewell. He discussed his funeral with me. His family were so upset that they had to be put to bed themselves. I went from his room to theirs from time to time, letting them know how he was.

Gradually, though, the man began to recover. Twenty-four hours, then forty-eight hours passed, and he began to take a new hold on life which strengthened daily. About a month later he was dismissed from the hospital. He was told to reduce his

activities and to re-order his plan of life. This he did,
and he lived five years longer. My own interpretation
of these facts is that having accepted the factual presence of death on faith in God, this man was given a
new lease on life.

3. Another facet of a legitimate and realistic faith
healing is that some people actually *decide to die.*
Their raison d'être *is not in this life.* Nor is this always
simply a manifestation of the "suicide" impulse as such.
Rather it may be the affirmation of a larger life. God's
methods of healing are not all finite ones and sometimes the "medicine of immortality" alone can heal.
For instance, I conferred one Sunday morning with a
sixty-three-year-old woman patient. She told me that
she was being dismissed that day by her doctor. She
was suffering from a mild arthritis and was "in for a
check-up." In the course of our brief chat she told me
that her husband had died three weeks before. One
week before, her only son had been committed to a
state hospital, and her "homestead" was to be sold to
pay off debts.

She asked me to pray for her and her son. I did so
and bade her good-bye. She took a walk down the hall
about half an hour later and dropped dead in the hall.
I was deeply moved by this and conferred with her
doctor. He said that he felt that she had no good reason for living and "*decided* to go on to her reward."
He reassured me by saying: "You and I have little

right to contest her decision. I think it was a good one!"

It is a fact, as far as I can discover, that there is a line in the course of many serious illnesses at which the *will to live* or the *decision to die* become quite determinative in the prognosis of the patient. It is at these points, then, that the man of faith functions as a healer. With tense, anxious, warring personalities, he actually calls something of a "contending spirit" *out of* the person. Then through an act of surrender the person "makes his peace" with the fact of his finitude, weakness, and limitation. He accepts death and gains life.

Harry M. Tiebout describes this in precise psychological concepts in his description of "the act of surrender in the treatment of the alcoholic." He defines this act of surrender as "a moment when the unconscious forces of defiance and grandiosity actually cease to function effectively. When that happens the individual is wide open to reality; he can listen and learn without conflict and fighting back. He is receptive to life, not antagonistic. He senses relatedness and an at-oneness which become the sources of an inner peace and serenity, the possession of which frees the individual from his compulsion to drink. In other words, an act of surrender is an occasion when the individual no longer fights life but accepts it." [1]

On the other hand, a pastor has to deal with the submissive, resigned, disheartened, and cast-down person. Here the man of faith functions as a "son of encouragement," putting "heart into" these persons. Thus they are made whole by reasons of their newfound faith at his hands. For a while, they actually draw upon his faith. He "perceives that strength goes out of him." Yet, if he is personally committed to God and responsibly related to God, and not exploitatively seeking to "use" and manipulate God as would a sorcerer, then his strength is like the widow's cruse of oil: it can be given without being depleted.

Paradoxically enough, however, the healer who has faith must also have faith in the right of the person to die if he chooses. Even Rogers suggests this when he says in his *Client-Centered Therapy:*

> To me it appears that only as the therapist is completely willing that *any* outcome, *any* direction, may be chosen—only then does he realize the vital strength of the capacity and potentiality of the individual for constructive action. It is as he is willing for death to be the choice, that life is chosen; for neuroticism to be the choice, that a healthy normality is chosen. The more completely he acts upon this central hypothesis, the more convincing is the evidence that the hypothesis is correct.[2]

A pastoral counselor, more specifically, is called upon to have faith enough in God, furthermore to know that healing itself is a finite and impermanent goal. God is greater than healing and to make healing the center and end of existence is to destroy the meaning of existence itself. It is to become an idolater, not far removed from the physical culture enthusiasts who worship at the shrine of the *young*, unblemished, and perfectly healthy body!

4. Another criterion for evaluating the validity of faith healing procedures is found in a psychological analysis of the way in which authority is used in the process of therapy. Authority has a large place in all healing. The word "authority" needs to be understood here in its more biblical meaning of "power" or "strength" or "virtue." All healing tends to take place in the context of an understood and accepted authority-relationship. Even nondirective therapy takes place in an authoritarian context in that the client comes to a counselor "who is *supposed to be good*," whose training gives him a certain "right" to practice his therapy. The exaggerated authority elements, however, in a faith healing relationship account for both the drama and the fickleness of results as compared with the less dramatic and more enduring changes effected in more permissive—but not necessarily less religious—healing relationships. Inherently, the *power* to heal has three sources: First, such power arises from a *healing community of concern*. The essence of this is described in the exhortation found in James 5:14-16:

Is any one among you suffering? Let him pray. Is any cheerful? Let him sing praise. Is any among you sick? Let him call for the elders of the church, and let them pray over him, anointing him with oil in the

name of the Lord; and the prayer of faith will save
the sick man, and the Lord will raise him up; and if
he has committed sins, he will be forgiven. Therefore
confess your sins to one another, and pray for one
another that you may be healed.

We know that people begin to languish in emotional
illness that takes its organic toll when they become
isolated from their meaningful community. The ter-
rible consequences of having no enduring community
of relatedness bore in upon Ananias to destroy him.
The power of communication with the body corporate
of believers "makes us whole." At the same time, the
power of *ex*communication of a significant community can destroy us. Alan Paton brilliantly describes
this destructiveness in his latest novel, *Too Late the
Phalarope*.

Healing within the framework of religious community, furthermore, rests upon some unquestioned authority in the faith healing relationship. The church
itself is a locus of authority. As has been seen in James
5:14-16, the effective authority of a harmonious Christian community at prayer in which the person is
wholeheartedly accepted is one source of healing
power. Likewise, the authority of a righteous man's
prayer wields "great power in its effects." Such a
community of understanding love undercuts the
sources of guilt, isolation, and loneliness that actually
can cause a person to languish in a loss of intention to
live. The power of forgiveness, communication, and

companionship sets at naught the forces of disease. These powers prevent disease; they arrest disease; they even reverse the course of disease.

The Catholic Church has institutionalized this community of healing, as indeed has Christian Science. Here rituals are developed, even as they were in Judaism for effective healing through ceremonial cleansing. Obedient participation in the authoritarian ritual purportedly—and often does—bring healing. The washings of Naaman and the pilgrims in the pool of Siloam are cases in point. Likewise, Jesus' command to the ten lepers to go show themselves to the priest is another example from within the Judaistic framework. The Asklepian cultic practices followed this ritualistic pattern. "The detailed procedures which were involved in the worship of Asklepios remain lost secrets of the priestly cult. Some items of the ceremonies used in healing have been reconstructed and can be summarized as follows: The sick person who desired aid through the ministrations of the god Asklepios was brought as a suppliant to the temple. He was prepared by a priest who told him of the power of the god and previous cures effected there. He was told to carry out certain preliminary rites, the nature of which is unknown except that these probably involved the making of sacrifices to Asklepios and perhaps Apollo." [3]

The Bible itself is a second source of authority, particularly for Protestant groups. The supportive min-

ister uses the strong reassurance of biblical passages.
(For example, see John Sutherland Bonnell's *Psychology for Pastor and People*.) The preaching pastor uses
the instruction of the Bible as his power, or authority.
The connection between faith and belief in "sound doctrine" is underlined in Titus. Here "sound doctrine"
comes from the same word from which we get our
word "hygiene" and may even be translated "health-
giving teaching." On the more spectacular side, but
more than this, the most vocal of the Protestant faith
healers base their appeal for power and authority to
heal on the infallible authority of the Scriptures. An
unusual example of this is described in a little book by
Oral Roberts, *If You Need Healing Do These
Things*.[4] The book has sold through the twelfth print-
ing 273,100 copies. The whole procedure is based
upon the literal interpretation of the Bible passages
on healing.

More tangible than these sources of authority is the
power of a sacred person, one endowed with the place
of a "man of God" in the life of a person. Couple this
powerful symbolic role with a sort of dashing, un-
hesitating decisiveness on the part of a person, and the
result is a person who has strong suggestive power. He
has *impact* upon others, and "commands" obedience of spirits of fear and bondage. Such an approach
does "rally" the real courage of a sick person, and
often accomplishes dramatic results in healing.

Quite regularly such healers consider themselves

gifted with a special "charisma" of healing. Thus authority rests in the personality of the healer by reason of a special charisma, or gift. Today such persons as Glenn Clark, Agnes Sanford, and others are among the best examples of such types of healing. In addition to their "gifts," they lay hold of certain medical facts such as those afforded by psychosomatic research. They couple these with such personal mystical experiences as they may have, thereby fashioning their healing methodology. Whereas scientific counselors tend to follow mystical "gifts" without saying so, these more ecstatic and mystical healers tend to follow more empirical ways of practicing their arts of healing without saying so. It is interesting also to observe that these healers make use of close-knit fellowship groups, such as The Camp Farthest Out groups, and that psychiatrists are showing great interest in therapeutic groups and communities.[5]

It is obvious, then, that authority of communities is concentrated in appointed personalities. Some attention needs to be given here to the degree, quality, and direction of the *authority* with which the healer is personally endowed. Healing comes to persons through faith because of their confidence in their healer. Even in the medical profession, we see certain secularized vestiges of faith healing in the patient's "confidence in his doctor." This need for authority is seen in bold relief in the passive-dependent persons who move from doctor to doctor seeking a placebo-like nostrum to heal them. The patient tells us, "*My* doctor is the *best* in the whole country. I swear by him." The psychoanalyst both requires confidence initially and seeks to add to it as he enjoins upon his patient to "trust" him completely and to say "whatever" comes into his mind. Lawrence S. Kubie, a psychoanalyst, in an article on psychoanalysis and healing by faith says that the "psychoanalyst expects and invites from his patients a frank and open skepticism." "Every effort is made in analytic therapy not to bind the patient to the analyst. . . ." The analyst "sets out not to exploit this uncritical worship but to analyze it away." However, Kubie's rather pious affirmations at this point may be true of the majority of psychoanalysts, but they do not tally with the actual practice of some psychoanalysts.

Furthermore, Kubie himself indicates in this article the authority-demand for a kind of "faith" in the analyst as a healer:

> Psychoanalysis demands confidence in the integrity and intelligence of the analyst, an intellectual willingness to co-operate, and a wholehearted purpose to abide by the rule of the analysis that the patient produce material freely and honestly. This in turn requires a courageous willingness to accept pain, anxiety, and deprivation, and to face unpleasant facts. Psychoanalysis, however, not only does not demand blind faith, it constantly attempts to analyze it away, even when this is faith in the analysis itself. Credulity impedes the

progress of analytic therapy and insight, by hiding secret disagreements under a mask of sham compliance.[6]

The major difference between psychoanalysis and faith healing, it seems, is that the faith healer "depends upon supernatural forces" and the psychoanalyst calls for confidence in himself. However, the kind of dependence or faith invested in the analyst is an "open-eyed" faith and not a blind credulity. This last statement is a "blind assertion" and not one backed up by careful research. We cannot accept it as so, just because Kubie says so. This is "blind faith."

Another aspect of the way in which authority appears in healing needs attention. The use of power may occasionally be reversed among faith healers to invoke harm upon persons. The authority of the Christian community, the authority of the Word of God, and the authority of the personage of the Apostle Peter not only healed the man at the Gate Beautiful, but they also destroyed Ananias. The isolation, the amputation from the only community he had, the feeling of condemnation from those "whose approval he considered most worthwhile" converged to destroy him. As the Apostle Paul put it:

> But thanks be unto God, who always leadeth us in triumph in Christ, and maketh manifest through us the savor of his knowledge in every place. For we are a sweet savor of Christ unto God, in them that are saved, and in them that perish; to the one a savor from death unto death; to the other a savor from life unto life.

And who is sufficient for these things? (II Corinthians 2:14-16)

A curious perversion of this today is the way in which cultic leaders, such as Father Divine, pronounce "curses" upon their antagonists. Furthermore, the climate of opinion is built up in certain circles that psychoanalysis is the *only* hope for *any* person to be healed. The negative inference of this is a sort of "pronounced doom" for the person who does not have the privilege of analysis.

Such use of power necessitates the continual re-examination of the healer's motives. The practice of faith healing has most often fallen into disrepute along the same lines of the great temptations of Jesus in the wilderness. The healer is tempted to use his practice as a means of base gain, of "turning stones into bread." The profit motive gets the best of him. Or, he may be enamored of the spectacular results of his first efforts For instance, the seventy returned to Jesus saying:

> Lord, even the devils are subject unto us through thy name. And he said unto them, I beheld Satan as lightning fall from heaven. Behold, I give unto you power to tread on serpents and scorpions, and over all the power of the enemy; and nothing shall by any means hurt you. Notwithstanding, in this rejoice not, that the spirits are subject unto you; but rather rejoice, because your names are written in heaven. (Luke 10:17-20)

(We are most eager to tell of our therapeutic successes and love to have those whom we heal to tell it. But Jesus had a way of charging his patients to tell no one.) Then finally, this may be a way of erotically extracting covert sexual gratification from other persons. According to John T. McNeill, these are the reefs upon which the cure of souls has been dashed too often.[7]

Therefore, the sincerity of any therapist may be tested by these criteria. One needs to ask about any healer: "Does he draw upon the purely finite motives for the authority to heal? Has the healer accepted the disciplines that the practice of healing demands?" As Jesus said to the disciples who had failed to heal the epileptic boy: "This kind cannot be driven out by anything but prayer." (Mark 9:29) The deceptiveness, the tawdriness of motive, and the insincerity of a counterfeit concern are all sensed and recognized by the diseased person sooner or later, and in the response of the demonic spirits to the seven sons of Sceva, the sick person is likely to say to fake healers: "Jesus I know, and Paul I know, but who are you?" (Acts 19:15) This will be true even if the healer repeats great religious truths as his "magic words." Sorcery may be defined as the use of the resources of the infinite to achieve a purely finite end. However, this is quite different from the secular healer who uses purely finite means to achieve purely finite ends, with no pretense of doing a thing in the name or power of God.

The use of authority and the necessity for sincerity in healing accent the degree of responsibility the faith healer takes for the results of the cure he offers. When asked how far in the use of "depth therapy" a minister should go, I have always answered: "He should go as far as his training, his limitations of time, and his willingness to accept responsibility for his treatment of a patient will permit him to go." This is an essentially ethical problem which also applies to the ecstatic and charismatic healers. Legal counterparts involve the healer, also.

The primary ethical problem in faith healing is that of receiving an accurate diagnosis of the illness and exhausting all *known* procedures for therapy as an act of faith in itself. Kubie rightly discerns that the treatment of disease which considers differential diagnosis as superfluous depends upon a faith that is blindly credulous. The faith healer who has no such information easily may say that *he* cured a cancer victim upon nothing more than the word of the patient himself! Of course general practitioners of medicine often take at face value the patient's own diagnoses, also.

Such differential diagnosis calls for the close cooperation between doctors and ministers because ministers have neither the training, the relationship, nor the equipment for diagnosis. This teamwork is the basis upon which pastoral psychology is built. However, to assume that *all* faith is summed up and epitomized and should be placed on the incomplete and partial wisdom of the doctor is to put him in God's place. We would not want to load him with such a crushing role in life, nor would we want to take his philosophical judgments at face value. He has neither the training, the relationship, nor the equipment to make these judgments unaided by ministers and theologians who spend their lives in these pursuits. But together they can form an effective healing team. Each of them has an ethical obligation to relate effectively to each other.

The second ethical problem of faith healing is that of the responsibility of the therapist for the safety and well-being of his patient. This problem is discussed to some extent by Willard Sperry in his book on *The Ethical Bases of Medical Practice* but not adequately enough. Medical doctors have such a heavy responsibility for the lives of their patients that in great numbers they carry "malpractice insurance" to protect them even in those instances where the most diligent efforts nevertheless leave them the victims of law suits.

But little has been done by ministers to devise a commonly acceptable standard of "counseling and therapeutic ethics" for the profession. Particularly is this true in the realm of faith healing. Legal responsibility for the death of a person who did not get medical care because of the religious scruples against doing

so taught by faith healers has not been clearly established. C. C. Cawley has written a gripping novel,
Fool's Haven, in which the mother of a deceased girl
was convicted of manslaughter for refusing to get
medical aid for her daughter. But the pastor who said,
"Her death was the will of God," went free. Cawley
feels that the time has come for society to reassess its
existing legal boundary between religious freedom and
fanatical religious irresponsibility.

This raises a whole issue about our legal responsibility, but it is a deeper one: of our personal responsibility for our stewardship of the power given to us by
God. The ministry is more than a profession, but it is
not less than a profession. We have this treasure in
earthen vessels in order that the excellency of the
power may be of God and not ourselves. We should
have our therapeutic code of ethics, too—a pastoral
equivalent of the Hippocratic oath. (At points this
overlaps with the need for a special code of ethics for
psychiatrists, also.)

Furthermore, an ethical issue is at stake in the failure of ministers to refer when referral is obviously indicated. Thus, the pastor assumes more responsibility
for healing than he has time to discharge, training to
effect, or conditions to control. But more than this, a
spiritually discerning "testing" of the spirits or motives of faith healers and "therapists" of every kind
should be devised by the Christian community itself.

To wait for the necessities of secular juries and judges to do it is to overlook the injunction of Scripture to settle such matters out of court. Also, negligence and timidity combine to cause us to avoid the leadership in such matters. We are enjoined to "test the spirits" to see whether they are of God, for many false prophets are gone out into the world.

They usually make healing itself their god, and thus become idolaters. They usually operate apart from a Christian community, as "free lancers," and they often exploit the people. The Christian community has yet, however, to find ways of distinguishing true healers from false ones. As a result, two conditions exist: Many charlatans take advantage of sincere people, and the vital relationship between faith and health is avoided by "sensible" religious folk. The pastoral counselor can do something about this if he develops a sound theology and ethic of healing, and embraces a consciously devised healing ethic which embodies criteria for distinguishing false healers from true ones.

Footnotes

1. *Pastoral Psychology*, Vol. I, No. 2, March, 1950, pp. 32-41.

2. Carl Rogers, *Client-Centered Therapy* (New York: Houghton Mifflin, 1951), pp. 48-49.

3. Spencer L. Rogers, "Psychotherapy in the Greek and Roman World," *Ciba Symposia*, Vol. 9, No. ½, April-May, 1947, p. 625.

4. (Tulsa, Oklahoma: Healing Waters, Inc., 1952).

5. See Maxwell Jones, *The Therapeutic Community* (New York: Basic Books, 1953).

6. *Pastoral Psychology*, Vol. I, No. 2, March, 1950, p. 15.

7. John T. McNeill, *A History of the Cure of Souls* (New York: Harper, 1951).

258
D683

DATE DUE

MAR 31 '82			
APR 13 '83			
MAY 11 '84			
MAY 10 '89			

DEMCO 38-297